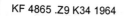

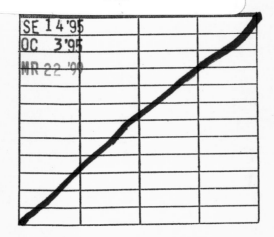

This

... is an authorized facsimile made from the master copy of the original book. Further unauthorized copying is prohibited.

Books on Demand is a publishing service of UMI. The program offers xerographic reprints of more than 130,000 books that are no longer in print.

The primary focus of Books on Demand is academic and professional resource materials originally published by university presses, academic societies, and trade book publishers worldwide.

RELIGION AND THE CONSTITUTION

Previously Published
in the Edward Douglass White Lecture Series

RELIGION
and the
CONSTITUTION

PAUL G. KAUPER

Louisiana State University Press · 1964

Copyright 1964 by
Louisiana State University Press

Library of Congress Catalog Card Number: 64–7898
Manufactured in the United States of America by
Kingsport Press, Inc., Kingsport, Tennessee

Designed by Jules B. McKee

PREFACE

This book consists of the Edward Douglass White Lectures which I was privileged to give at Louisiana State University in March, 1964. In accordance with the lecture committee's suggestion, I devoted the three lectures to a discussion of contemporary questions respecting religion in its relation to the constitutional order. Religious, sociological, and constitutional developments, as I point out in the first chapter, have all contributed to lend new significance to problems of the interrelationship of law and religion. In these lectures I have attempted to delineate basic considerations relevant to this interrelationship in the context of the contemporary scene.

Chapters Two and Three are concerned primarily with the underlying constitutional issues. The First Amendment, which says that Congress shall make no laws respecting an establishment of religion or prohibiting the free exercise thereof, states two ideas which find their basic unity in the concept of religious liberty as broadly understood to include freedom of belief and conscience in its largest sense. These two ideas often converge harmoniously on the same result, but in some situations they compete with each other. How far can the government's role in protecting and promoting religious liberty be pushed without violating the establishment limitation, and how far can the establishment limitation be pushed without violating religious liberty?

In the second chapter I deal with religious liberty as the central facet of the constitutional problem. Is religious liberty really an independent substantive liberty or is it one aspect of a broader freedom of expression? Why should religious liberty be recognized as an independent liberty? How shall religious belief be defined? What are the dimensions of religious liberty, and what limitations may properly be placed on it? Does it occupy a preferred place in the scheme of constitutional values, and does the legislature have either the duty or the discretionary freedom to take positive steps in granting various kinds of exemptions on religious grounds?

The establishment clause and the interpretations placed upon it furnish the critical point in discussion of current issues. Separation of church and state as a constitutional principle rests primarily on this clause. As pointed out in the third chapter, three principal theories appear in the Supreme Court's opinions on the interpretations of the establishment language: (1) the no-aid or strict separation theory, (2) the strict neutrality theory, and (3) the accommodation theory. The Supreme Court has not yet fully committed itself to an overall rationale or theory, but it seems to me that interpretation of the establishment limitation with an eye to accommodation of religious liberty and the religious interests and needs of our people best explains the American development and offers a viable approach in reconciling the free exercise and establishment limitations. The problems we face cannot be solved by simple rules or absolute propositions. The accommodation theory recognizes the task of the judiciary in arriving at judgment by weighing a variety of considerations.

In the concluding chapter I examine the implications of constitutional doctrine with respect to problems of current interest to the churches. First, how do the churches adjust themselves to the conditions of contemporary religious pluralism? What is their role in contributing to the national consensus and ethos? How do they make their witness relevant to the common life? And, in turn, what can the government do in recognizing the relevancy of religion to our national life? Can it be so completely secular that it is subject to the charge of promoting a secularistic philosophy? Since public schools may not prescribe religious practices, what can they do to recognize the relevance of religion in the educational process? The second large question centers on government support of church-related activities. With increasing governmental involvement in social welfare programs, what is the place of church-related institutions in these fields? The parochial school problem and the complex considerations relevant to it are discussed at this point. In concluding this chapter I suggest the perils to the churches if they accept government assistance at the expense of compromising their voluntaristic position and becoming identified as quasi-governmental agencies.

In dealing with these subjects, as briefly summarized above, I have necessarily painted with a broad brush. My concern has been to present ideas basic to the current debates rather than to deal with specific problems in detail. If these lectures, now made available to a wider audience, help define the issues and the considerations relevant to their resolution, they will have served a useful purpose.

This book conforms substantially to the lectures as originally delivered, although some portions of them as here reproduced were omitted in the course of lecturing because of a lack of time.

In documenting these lectures I have avoided extensive foot-notes and have kept references to a minimum by citing for the most part only the primary sources. Although some secondary sources are cited, I have not attempted to supply all relevant literature. In justice to those who have contributed to the wealth of literature in this field and because of the interest that a reader may have in exploring further, I have prepared a select bibliography at the end of the book.

I cannot conclude this preface without taking the opportunity to thank the Department of Government and the Law School of Louisiana State University for so kindly extending to me the privilege of delivering the 1964 Edward Douglass White Lec-tures and to acknowledge with gratitude the warm and generous hospitality extended to my wife and me during the course of our stay on the campus. We are especially grateful to Dean and Mrs. Paul M. Hebert, Associate Dean and Mrs. Milton M. Harrison, Professor and Mrs. Joseph Dainow, and Professor and Mrs. Wex S. Malone.

I acknowledge my indebtedness also to my assistant Mrs. Virginia Nordby for her valuable help in the preparation, edit-ing, and checking of the manuscript.

PAUL G. KAUPER

Ann Arbor, Michigan
June, 1964

CONTENTS

RELIGION AND THE CONSTITUTION

1

SOME INTRODUCTORY
CONSIDERATIONS

It is appropriate at the outset to say a word about the terminology employed in the general title. It is common these days to use the term "church-state" to embrace all questions that arise under our Constitution respecting religious freedom, the relation of law and religion, and the relation of churches and governments. Although this terminology has its usefulness as a shortcut and as a symbol of current problems, it suffers from weaknesses and inadequacies. Church-state terminology comes to us from Europe and recalls a background which is quite unlike the American scene. It had its origin in a time when the church was indeed a single monolithic Church and governmental power was centered in a single ruler. It is inadequate to describe the American situation because of both the multitude of churches in this country and the dispersion of governmental power among the federal government, the states, and the local communities.

In our situation, it is more illuminating to call them problems of the interrelationship of the civil and the religious communities. This phrase at least makes clear that we are discussing communities that embrace in part a common membership. Some implications with respect to separateness are immediately seen. The difficulty in the use of church-state terminology is that it at once creates a picture of two competing power structures and suggests a clear line that marks their separate functions. Indeed, a literal application of the separation idea is often invoked by the use of a metaphor—"a wall of separation between church and state." Although we do recognize a separateness of the functions of civil and ecclesiastical authorities—thereby recognizing the principle of separation of church and state—we cannot understand the problem without considering numerous interacting areas of function and interest.

An even more fundamental difficulty in the common use of church-state terminology is that it is inadequate to describe the totality of current problems. Our interest extends to the entire interrelationship of law and religion. Formal relations between the churches as institutions and the government are only one part of this whole problem. Church-state relations, it may be suggested, embrace only the questions that are peculiar to the interrelationship of government and churches. This includes such questions as representation by government in the affairs of the churches and, in turn, representation by churches in the affairs of government; the control by either of the other; the levying of taxes by the government to support church activities as well as tax exemptions for churches; the freedom of the churches in their corporate capacity to give witness to faith by speaking out in matters of governmental concern; the jurisdiction of civil courts in ecclesiastical matters and the effect of the adjudications of ecclesiastical tribunals. To describe these problems as church-state relations is meaningful.

There are, however, larger questions extending to the relation of law and religion. We may mention, for instance, the impact of religious ideas upon the law, the protection and advancement of religious liberty through the institutions and processes of government, the granting under law of special privileges based on religious grounds, the use of public funds and facilities to aid religious purposes, and the use of government power to sanction religious beliefs and practices. The influence of churches on governmental policy may often lurk in the background of some of these problems. Nevertheless, it is useful to analyze whether in a given case we are talking about a church-state relationship or whether we are talking about law in relation to religion.

The following chapters embrace a variety of questions centered on religion and its constitutional limitations. The second chapter is directed to an examination of religious liberty as the central facet of the constitutional law problem. In the third chapter the theories developed by the Supreme Court in interpreting the establishment limitation of the First Amendment and its relationship to the free exercise guarantee are examined. In the fourth chapter the implications of constitutional doctrine are considered in the light of our contemporary religious pluralism, and some specific problems concerning religion in public life and the use of governmental funds to support church welfare and educational activities are discussed. The central emphasis will be on the Constitution of the United States, as a limitation on both the federal government and the states. Some reference will necessarily also be made, however, to state constitutions, which too frequently are neglected in any study of these problems but which are very useful: their historical development, the concreteness of the provisions commonly found in them, and the interpretations based on them help supply perspective and contribute relevant ideas.

The choice of subject for these lectures, in response to the lecture committee's suggestion, attests the new and enlarged interest in these problems shared by lawyers, churchmen, and the general public. This is a very recent development. An important factor generating the contemporary discussion is the series of Supreme Court cases culminating in the recent decisions that Bible-reading and prayer exercises in public schools are invalid.[1] These decisions and the interpretations of the First Amendment supporting them have opened up areas of inquiry of great concern to everyone. But constitutional development does not move in a vacuum, and I suggest that the new judicial interpretations and the problems raised by them must be seen in the context of socio-religious and political developments which give new meaning to the issues raised before the courts.

One need not dig far into the literature of our day to appreciate the awareness of religious leaders and sociologists that a very substantial change has taken place in the configuration of American religious life. The emergence of contemporary religious pluralism is central to this change.[2] It is now clear that no one religious group in this country can claim a dominant position in American life. Protestant domination of the national religious life from early days through the first decades of this century has come to an end. This change has resulted in large part from the tides of immigrants who have augmented the strength of the Catholic and Jewish communities. A striking feature of the change in religious patterns has been the rise of Catholicism to a new position of importance in American life. The election of John F. Kennedy as President in 1960 dramatically symbolized the claim of Catholics to speak with equal voice in our national life. During this same period the Jewish community has consolidated its position as a strong and articulate minority sharing an equal position with the Protestant and Catholic churches. The contemporary situation is often described in terms of the tripartite religious division as developed in Will Herberg's *Protestant, Catholic and Jew.*

Herberg's tripartite classification is useful for some purposes, yet it is not adequate to describe the diversity embraced by our contemporary religious pluralism. The nation's religions embrace a number of minority groups not included in the three major faiths. Moreover, the picture of religious pluralism is incomplete without reference to unbelievers, agnostics, the unchurched, and a wide variety of secular faiths and ideologies that seek to lay claim to men's loyalties. Implicit in the demands of contemporary religious pluralism is not only a recognition of the place and influence of the major faiths, but also a sensitivity to and respect for minority groups and all varieties of belief.

The new religious pluralism raises questions for the churches. First, what is the relation of these groups to each other? All religions lay claim to ultimate truth, and they compete for men's minds and souls. How do they stand with respect to each other? Do they generate tension because of their competitive positions and merely seek to accommodate themselves to the maintenance of civic peace? Or do they advance in mutual respect and cooperation, seeking by dialogue and common discussion to understand not only their differences, but also their common interests and goals? Perhaps an answer to this question is found in the great ecumenical movement of our day. Not only are Protestant churches moving toward greater unity, but equally important are the ecumenical stirrings within all Christendom—especially the movement for understanding between the Protestant and Catholic communities. Now also for the first time Jewish, Protestant, and Catholic religious leaders and scholars are examining each other's faiths in a new venture of respect and understanding. A major concern of these three groups pertains to the problems discussed in this book. Both the Protestant and Jewish communities still share some doubt as to whether Catholicism is fully committed to religious liberty. The Jewish community in particular—mindful of a long history of persecution and second-class religious status—stands resolutely for a minimum involvement of government in religious matters. Exploration of a possible consensus on constitutional issues is itself one of the striking features of current interfaith discussions.

Contemporary religious pluralism also raises the critical question of the relation of the several religious groups and the faiths they espouse to the national life. It has generally been assumed in the past that religion supplies a cohesive and unifying force for the social community and by shaping mores contributes to the common faith and purpose of the community. No single religion is in a position to supply that cohesive force today. Where then do the churches stand? What contributions, if any, do the churches make to the common life, if none is in a position to dominate and shape the ethos underlying the public consensus? Is there, indeed, any means by which the religious groups can achieve some consensus in a national faith? Or is the matter of religion now irrelevant to public life? Do the churches retreat into a wholly sectarian position unrelated to the public order? Does the church as a spiritual community make its impact on the common ethos through the spiritual and moral leavening of individuals who translate their faith into civic virtue and understanding? Do the churches have a corporate witness to make on matters of community concern, and can they do so without being charged with attempting to use the law and its processes to achieve sectarian or political ends? In turn, is it the object of the churches to unite in some common-denominator faith or some common body of moral values that will lay the foundation for a community ethos?

At this point we may note another feature of American life that has accompanied the emergence of the new pluralism:

religion has enjoyed great popularity in this country in postwar years. Church membership has risen to a new high. The statistics show a high rate of church attendance, and the churches have prospered financially. If nothing else, religion has become highly respectable. A concomitant feature has been the tendency to identify religion with "Americanism" and the "American way of life." Is this kind of syncretistic folk cult the answer to the quest for consensus? Is this the logical outcome of attempts to find a common-denominator faith or a common core of moral values that would lay the foundation of an unofficially established national religion? The perils to the historic faiths are manifest if they witness to such a vague religiosity and if such a folk religion is identified with the public order, the law, and public institutions.

What, in turn, is the response of the state to the new pluralism? Should the government, in the interest of preserving the civic peace not only among the religious groups but also between the religious groups and the nonreligious groups, more than ever abstain from any involvement in religious matters and yet at the same time exercise its powers more effectively to promote religious liberty and the freedom of all persons and groups to bear witness to their faith and proclaim their message? But does the heightened necessity of maintaining religious liberty and religious neutrality force government to secularize itself so completely that it ignores the relevance of religion in the national life and in the lives of its citizens? Does the process of further secularization of the public order thereby make the government a party to the promotion of a secularistic orientation which becomes the officially established faith?

I have raised this series of questions to suggest the implications of contemporary pluralism not only with respect to the position of the churches in relation to each other and in relation to the common life, but also with respect to governmental policy and the constitutional order. The recent Supreme Court decisions cannot be fully appraised without reference to the fundamental changes and movements in American religious life.

The second important development that has forced a re-examination of church-state problems is the expansion of the government's role in all areas of American life. This is particularly true of the federal government and its activities. We are now living in the era of the expanding welfare state when government is assuming constantly broader authority in its spending, tax, and regulatory powers to meet human needs. This means that government is encroaching on areas of social concern that were at one time the special responsibility of vol-untaristic societies, particularly the churches. The churches, as an expression of their concern for human needs and in witness to their faith, have conducted a variety of welfare and chari-table activities. They have also engaged in educational enter-prises at all levels. The assumption by government of an increased responsibility for educational and welfare needs, the inability of the churches and other voluntaristic groups to meet these needs, and the growing financial burden on private insti-tutions in maintaining their programs—all pose serious ques-tions for both the churches and the government. Can and should the churches continue to engage in their own welfare and educational programs? Should the government recognize the concurrent role of voluntaristic associations in these programs and lend them financial support? Can the churches accept such assistance without compromising their religious and volun-taristic character? These questions lead to problems of vital concern respecting the constitutionality and propriety of gov-ernmental assistance to schools and colleges and to hospitals and other welfare enterprises conducted under church auspices.

A conspicuous concomitant feature of this development has been the greater concentration of power in the national government and a greater awareness of the national interest in these matters. Not only is the federal government expanding its legislative authority in dealing with these problems as matters of national concern, but the Supreme Court of the United States through its interpretation of the Fourteenth Amendment is continually extending federal limitations on local action. At one time the question of whether or not a local school board could require Bible-reading or prayer exercises was not a matter that attracted national attention nor was it even thought to raise a national constitutional question. This has changed. The Supreme Court's broadened interpretations of the Fourteenth Amendment as a restriction on state actions—evident in such cases as the released time, Bible-reading, and prayer cases—are all symptomatic of a decline of localism and an awareness of a larger national interest in these matters. Yet this development is also a source of controversy and difficulty in a federal system where retention of a degree of local autonomy is considered to be a vital and important social factor. The problem is compounded because the religious pluralism which is so clearly evident on the national level and contributes to the shaping of national policy is not always reflected on the local scene.

The developments I have briefly outlined here have provoked new thought, study, and soul-searching by the religious groups in this country: they are trying to determine their position not only on questions relating to constitutional policy and the Supreme Court's decisions, but also on the more basic question of their own policy toward the role of government in religious matters. Religious groups are asking whether they need to take a fresh look at many historically sanctioned usages which may not be compatible either with what the Supreme Court has said our Constitution requires or with the demands of our contemporary society. All the churches are examining their position on the whole question of religious liberty, of church-state relations, and of the propriety of accepting governmental aid for various purposes germane to their own activities.

This process of self-examination is proving to be particularly acute for the Protestant churches. No longer a dominant group in this country, they are now forced to redefine their contribution to the common life, their relationship to the other religious communities, and their relationship to government. It is fair to say that Protestant thinking is governed in part by a question of strategy in meeting what is felt to be the new power of the Catholic church in this country. The fear persists that the Catholic church has not fully committed itself to American concepts of religious liberty and of separation of church and state. But the Protestant self-examination is in part also a soul-searching in which the churches are asking themselves if as a matter of religious principle and conviction they should adopt a wholly voluntaristic position and divorce themselves from anything that evidences reliance upon governmental aid and assistance. Or should they attempt to define a viable middle way in areas of common concern? [3]

2

RELIGIOUS LIBERTY:

Some Basic
Considerations

Religious liberty is chosen as the starting point of this discussion for two reasons. In the first place, I propose the thesis that religious liberty is the central concern of the constitutional order as it relates to the subject of religion. The purpose of the constitutional system—both in the restriction it imposes on the power of the government to interfere with the free exercise of religion and the limitation on the power of government to establish, aid, and support religion—is to protect and promote religious liberty in the widest sense of the term, including the individual's freedom to believe and to express his belief and the liberty of religious communities to bear witness to the truth they confess. In this view religious liberty is the central purpose served by the principle of separation of church and state.

Secondly, we have a substantial body of constitutional provisions and judicial interpretations which have defined the meaning of religious liberty and its free exercise and which, in turn, contribute to the understanding of the constitutional provisions prohibiting use of governmental power to support religious activities. The guarantee of religious liberty is a characteristic feature of American constitutions. It finds expression in the provision of the First Amendment which says that Congress shall make no law respecting an establishment of religion or prohibiting the free exercise thereof.[1] It also finds expression in our state constitutions. Although they differ in detail, they commonly include provisions that every person shall be at liberty to worship God according to the dictates of his own conscience,[2] that the civil and political rights of no person shall be abridged or diminished on account of his religious belief,[3] that no person shall be required to contribute to the erection or support of any place of religious worship or to pay tithes, taxes, or other rates for the support of any minister of the gospel or teacher of religion.[4] Many contain the further provisions that either no sectarian instruction shall be permitted in the public schools or that these schools shall be free of sectarian control,[5] and that public funds shall not be used in support of sectarian education or religious institutions.[6] It is useful at this point to note that in the state constitutions the provisions against the use of public funds for sectarian education or for religious purposes are intimately bound up with provisions guaranteeing freedom of worship, and they suggest that in the American view it is a violation of religious liberty to compel people to pay taxes to support religious activities or institutions.

These provisions, in turn, must be viewed in the light of historical circumstances and the struggle that culminated in the latter part of the eighteenth century against continuing a system whereby all persons were required to pay taxes to support either the established religion or religious ministers of their own persuasion. This is not to suggest that the full concept of religious liberty as it has come to be interpreted in American life is found in the constitutional texts. Their implications have been developed by the process of judicial decision, particularly the decisions interpreting the free exercise clause of the First Amendment, which applies directly to Congress but which by judicial interpretation of the Fourteenth Amendment has been made applicable to the states as well. The important point is that religious liberty is recognized as an independent substantive liberty, having its own purpose, content, and dimension and existing apart from the other commonly recognized guarantees of free speech, free press, and freedom of assembly.

Although religious liberty in its several facets is recognized in the constitutions as an independent liberty, some have advanced the proposition that it is not a separate category of substantive freedom but is embraced in the freedoms of speech, press, and assembly. Admittedly, religious freedom is easily identifiable in many situations with these other freedoms, and there is on the surface a plausible basis for merging religious freedom with them. A person's liberty to express his religious belief can be construed as free speech or free press, and a person's freedom from coercion of belief can be formulated in terms of a general intellectual liberty distilled from these other freedoms. Attention is called to the decision by the United States Supreme Court in the *Barnette* case holding that a school board could not compel a Jehovah's Witness child to take part in a flag salute exercise.[7] This decision was not grounded on religious freedom but rather on the ground that the First Amendment secures a general right to be free from state compulsion to accept any particular creed or ideology.

The most persuasive case in support of the idea that religious liberty does not enjoy an independent status under the First Amendment has been stated by Professor Philip Kurland of the University of Chicago law school.[8] He has advanced the thesis that the establishment and free exercise clauses of the First Amendment, rather than stating independent substantive limitations on the federal government, are properly construed to state a unified and coherent rationale more aptly described in equal protection terms. According to this conception the underlying purpose implicit in the religion clauses of the First Amendment is that the religious factor shall not be used as the basis of a legislative classification designed either to hinder or promote religious activities. In short, these clauses are designed to prohibit government from subjecting religion to discriminatory treatment and from according it a preferred treatment. As Professor Kurland sees it, the basic expression of religious beliefs is embraced in the freedom of speech, press, and assembly. Therefore, religious liberty under the free exercise clause means that no person shall be disadvantaged because of religion in the exercise of these other freedoms or, indeed, in the enjoyment of any rights, privileges, or immunities secured by law and that, in turn, no person shall because of his religion enjoy an advantage under the law over and above that enjoyed by other people.

This is an interesting and arresting thesis. It goes to the heart of the question of what is meant by religious liberty and has many implications for questions of current interest. If this thesis is correct, there is no valid basis for judicial recognition of religious liberty as a preferred liberty under the constitutional system, no foundation for legislative exemptions from laws on religious grounds, no ground for treating church bodies differently from other voluntary associations. In turn, this thesis means that government in the dispensation of public funds may not use the religious factor as a basis for discriminatory treatment. Thus, if government makes grants or loans to all hospitals generally, including those under private control, it may not, according to this view, withhold such assistance from church-related hospitals.

Certainly it must be acknowledged that many cases involving the expression of religious belief or involving the corporate activities of churches can be decided on grounds that are not peculiar to religious liberty, such as freedom of speech, press, and assembly or the freedom of association which is recognized as implicit in the First Amendment and in the liberty secured by the due process clause. It should be clear also that as a general proposition an individual should not be discriminated against in the enjoyment of any right, privilege, or immunity because of his religious belief. Freedom from discrimination on religious grounds should be a facet of religious liberty. Likewise, as a general proposition, no person should be allowed to claim that because of his religion he is entitled as a matter of constitutional right to claim an exemption from general regulatory and tax laws. But conceding all this, it is still fair to say that our whole constitutional history refutes the argument that what is meant by religious liberty is a principle directed against preferential or discriminatory treatment on religious grounds. Rather, it supports the conclusion that religious liberty is an independent liberty, that its recognition may either require or permit preferential treatment on religious grounds in some instances, and that it does not necessarily preclude discrimination on religious grounds in certain situations.

As previously pointed out, religious liberty is not only spelled out in the free exercise clause of the First Amendment but is explicitly recognized in its various concrete facets in the state constitutions, where it is usually the subject of a separate article or paragraph or otherwise receives special consideration. The specific identification in a bill of rights of freedom to worship, freedom from disability on religious grounds, freedom from taxes to support ministers of religion and houses of worship as important freedoms worthy of constitutional recognition cannot be ignored. Nor can we ignore the decisions by the United States Supreme Court which rest on explicit recognition of religious liberty as a substantive freedom under the First Amendment, even though some of these decisions might have rested on grounds consistent with Professor Kurland's thesis.[9] Moreover, as will be pointed out later, our constitutional history supports the proposition that the religious factor may in some situations be a basis for special classification resulting in either preferential or discriminatory treatment. State constitutions commonly require or authorize tax exemptions for property used for a house of worship or other religious purposes.[10] Congress and the state legislatures have proceeded on the assumption that they enjoy some discretionary authority to use the religious factor as the basis for preferential treatment. Federal and state statutes involving either the taxing or the regulatory powers grant exemptions because of religious belief or religious activity.[11]

On the other hand, history supports the proposition that for some purposes the religious factor may be used as a ground for discrimination in public privilege or common right. The most notable example is the provision commonly found in state constitutions prohibiting the use of public funds in support of sectarian schools.[12] These provisions have been construed by some state courts to prohibit not only the use of public funds to support parochial schools,[13] but also the use of such funds to provide secular textbooks for children in parochial schools [14] and bus transportation for children going to parochial schools.[15] Insofar as these provisions deny the use of public funds to support parochial schools, while the state is free to support all other schools—public and private—which satisfy the requirement of the compulsory education laws, they clearly discriminate on religious grounds in the dispensation of public funds.

The use of the word discrimination these days suggests something odious or evil. But at this point I am not suggesting that the kinds of discrimination mentioned above are evil or that there are no concepts of public policy to support these classifications. The point to be underscored here is that the religious factor in our constitutional tradition has received both preferential and discriminatory classifications, and that any principle of classification in religion cannot be understood unless religious liberty is considered an independent liberty in a total context of religious considerations.

The decisions by the United States Supreme Court interpreting the free exercise clause of the First Amendment also indicate that religious liberty has its own dimensions and is not to be identified in terms solely of a classification principle. To be sure, there are decisions by the Supreme Court which uphold the right of a particular religious group to use public parks for worship, where the decisions rested on a finding of discrimination against the group by law enforcement officers or licensing officials.[16] There are also decisions upholding the right of persons to distribute religious literature, which rested on free speech and not peculiarly on religious freedom.[17] On the other hand, some of the court's decisions, notably those relating to Jehovah's Witnesses, have rested on the ground of religious liberty [18] and, indeed, in some instances, have accorded religious liberty a higher degree of constitutional protection than that accorded free speech and free press generally.[19] The distribution and sale of religious literature as a proselytizing activity enjoys a special immunity to local license taxes applicable to salesmen and vendors,[20] and house-to-house

solicitation for religious purposes enjoys a preferred immunity to ordinances regulating these activities in the interest of household privacy.[21]

Perhaps the most notable example of the Supreme Court's recognition that religious liberty furnishes a basis for preferred treatment is found in the recent decision of *Sherbert* v. *Verner*.[22] The court held that the free exercise clause requires a state to recognize a religious ground (namely, the duty of Seventh-Day Adventists not to work on Saturday) as the basis for a special exemption from the provision of an unemployment compensation law which makes a person ineligible for compensation if he refuses a job for which he is qualified. This decision makes it clear that in some instances the legislature is required to grant a special exemption on religious grounds from laws of general application in order not to burden the free exercise of religion.

Review of constitutional provisions and court decisions makes abundantly clear that religious liberty occupies a separate and special position among our constitutionally protected liberties. To reinforce this point further, one may point to the constitutions of other countries—particularly those that have been adopted since World War II—in which religious liberty, often coupled with freedom of conscience or freedom of ideological expression, is recognized as a special liberty, apart from the other recognized freedoms of expression.[23]

Why should we have this singling out and even preferred treatment of religious liberty when freedom of religious thought and activity appears to be adequately encompassed within other freedoms of broader range? Why should distinctively religious concern not be confined to the problem of discrimination? Various considerations are pertinent to this inquiry—the long struggle for the recognition of religious liberty, the history of religious persecution and of wars fought over religious domination and conformity, and the exploitation of governmental power by ecclesiastical authorities to suppress dissent and freedom of thought. Surely they played their part in the final victory for religious liberty and the recognition that freedom is a seamless web and that when religious liberty is imperiled, free speech, free press, and the total liberty of the person are at stake. Yet I suggest that there is something peculiar and fundamental to religion which gives religious liberty a distinctive character and places religious institutions in a separate category.[24]

The separate basis for religious liberty is more readily understood if we examine the arguments advanced in support of free speech, using that term in a wide sense to include speech, press, and assembly. Some find free speech essential to the projection of human personality and the opportunity for self-fulfillment. To others, free speech—viewed as a socially utilitarian value—is the necessary condition for arriving at truth in the market place, to use Justice Holmes's familiar expression.[25] Others regard free speech as the indispensable condition of our democratic order, since without the freedom of dissent and the opportunity for all to take part in the great public debate, as Professor Alexander Meiklejohn has said, democracy loses its central core.[26] According to this view free speech has its highest value when it means the freedom to speak out on matters of public concern.

These bases for free speech indicate why freedom of religion cannot be completely identified with free speech or merged with it so as to lose its own significance. To be sure, religious expression can be identified with expression of the personality; it can be seen as a contribution to the common discussion necessary to arrive at truth; it can be viewed as a means of expression on matters of common concern in our democratic society, and to this extent it can be identified with the purposes served by a generalized freedom of expression. Yet I venture that these considerations do not embrace the central core of religious liberty, and this central core can be understood only by reference to the essential nature of religious belief and feeling.

Religion deals with man's relationship to his God, however he may be defined. It is a highly personal matter and involves a man's loyalty to God as his highest good and the duties arising from this relationship. It defines an area of spiritual autonomy which is withdrawn from the reach of civil authority. It involves belief, and it conditions conscience and feeling. It presupposes freedom and voluntary adherence and cannot be coerced. Classical Christian thinking supports this view. Christian theologians recognize, first of all, a basic interior freedom of the Christian that can be described only in spiritual terms and which by its nature is incapable of limitation or circumscription by the state.[27] This type of strictly interior freedom is not to be confused with religious liberty as a civic freedom. But Christians have also expressed the necessity of religious liberty as a civic freedom to protect their basic spiritual freedom.[28] Because Christians feel a duty and a compulsion to witness to their faith, they see that religious liberty affects their own spiritual commitment. As the Apostle Peter said, "We must obey God rather than men." [29] Moreover, in the best of Christian thought, religious liberty is essential because the Christian faith is not to be achieved by coercive power but by the working of the spirit of God.

Faith is the free gift of God: a man must be free to accept or reject it. It cannot be coerced by the power of the state. Freedom for all—whether believer or nonbeliever—is therefore implicit in the Christian view of religious faith. Moreover, because the Christian commitment requires witnessing to the faith, the free expression of this faith in word and deed is essential to the freedom of faith. Finally, since this faith is cultivated in the communion of believers and finds further expression in the corporate acts of this communion—also seen to rest on divine authority—the freedom of the church as a distinctive institution is equally necessary. The Christian view of man and his secular government must also be considered: because man is self-centered and sinful, he tends to reach out for power, but he has only limited wisdom in exercising power. Christian thought therefore reveals a skepticism about governmental authority that strengthens the case for religious liberty. Government is not capable of determining ultimate truth, and for this reason is precluded from sanctioning what it regards as religious truth.[30] Moreover, the human tendency to abuse power makes it essential that civic freedoms be recognized and maintained as the necessary conditions of the individual's freedom as a spiritual creature.

Christian thought translates religious liberty into a civic freedom that denies the state authority to prescribe what is true in religion, to compel acceptance of religious belief, or to interfere with the free expression of religious belief except when necessary to preserve peace and good order or to protect the freedoms of others. Indeed, the duty of the state with respect to religious matters is to maintain the conditions of peace, order, and freedom that promote freedom of faith in its fullest sense. The state's functions are directed to secular ends. It is not its business to intrude into the kingdom of the spirit.

I realize that I have distilled what I regard as best in Christian thought concerning religious liberty. Christians and their churches have not always adhered to this view, which has been most fully developed and accepted by Protestants. The Catholic church has not fully committed itself to a concept of religious liberty that denies the state's power to recognize and support religious truth.[31] It is lamentable that religious wars have been fought in the name of Christ and that Christian ecclesiastical authority has captured secular power in order to force religion on dissenters and nonconformists and to punish heretics. Even today there are countries under Christian domination where religious liberty is not enjoyed. Indeed, it is a distortion of history to say that the recognition of religious liberty in the Western world is peculiarly the contribution of Christian thought.

A second element, arising from the secular humanism of the Reformation and the Enlightenment, and finding expression in the United States in the views of Thomas Jefferson and James Madison, has contributed powerfully to the modern acceptance of religious liberty. This secular view, while reflecting also the Protestant right of dissent, is premised solidly on a recognition of the secular character of government, its incompetence and lack of jurisdiction over religious matters which belong to the private sphere, and the assumption that so far as the government is concerned, all religious truth is relative, and for this reason none can lay claim to governmental support and sanction. Its concern is with the freedom of dissent, freedom from government coercion of belief, and freedom of government from ecclesiastical aggrandizement. In this view, both government and religion flourish best when their separateness of function is maintained.[32]

The foregoing discussion has presupposed certain assumptions about the nature of religion and religious beliefs. But how religion is to be defined for constitutional purposes is a problem that requires further consideration.[33] To attempt a definition of religion is, indeed, presumptuous. Theologians, philosophers, and moralists cannot agree on a comprehensive definition. Its very nature eludes definition. Yet courts must define the meaning of religion for constitutional and other legal purposes, a task compounded in its difficulty since judges and lawyers cannot be presumed to have any particular competence with respect to religion. The question may well be raised: How can a secular court, composed of law-trained persons, give meaning to a constitutional clause respecting religion without at the same time understanding the nature of religion?

Obviously the judicial decisions that define the scope of religious liberty must make some assumptions as to the meaning of religion. When the United States Supreme Court says that freedom of religion includes the freedom to proselytize,[34] to use public streets for distribution of literature,[35] and to use public parks for worship,[36] that it includes freedom from religious tests for public office,[37] freedom from compulsion to engage in a flag salute exercise,[38] and freedom to conduct the affairs of a religious body without intervention by state legislature or state courts,[39] there must be some judicial understanding of what is meant by religion. Fortunately, the problems that have come before the court have not required a definitive judicial formulation of the meaning of religion that applies in all situations. Courts face concrete problems arising under a constitution or statute, and according to the traditions of case law, it is enough to define the problem for the purpose of the case. Moreover, most of the cases involving religious liberty deal with overt actions inspired by religious belief where the question is not whether the action is an expression of religious faith but whether it falls within the concept of the free exercise of religion, and if it does, whether it may still be subject to limitations imposed by law in the public interest. Even here the question is relevant whether the overt conduct can be characterized as religious conduct and presupposes a judicial understanding of the full measure of religious commitment. But in the usual case the court at least is spared the necessity of inquiring whether the underlying belief is religious in character. It is clear then that the distinction between belief and action is highly relevant in assessing the judicial task of defining religion. This distinction was succinctly brought home in Mr. Justice Robert's statement in *Cantwell* v. *Connecticut* that freedom of belief by its nature is absolute, whereas the freedom to engage in religious action is relative and limited.[40]

A second proposition is that having identified belief as religious, a court is not competent to pass on its truthfulness or validity. Not only is religious truth by its nature not subject to a test of validity determined by rational thought and empiric knowledge, but a principal purpose underlying religious liberty is to remove the question of what is true religion from the domain of the secular authority. This was made clear by the Supreme Court in the case of *United States* v. *Ballard,* where it was charged that the defendant had made fraudulent claims respecting religion in soliciting contributions through the federal mails.[41] The court wisely said that the truthfulness of the belief could not be an issue before the jury; this was a matter beyond the competence of a civil tribunal. The court did hold, however, that for the purpose of the federal fraud statute it was proper for the jury to consider whether the defendant was honest in claiming religious sanction for his belief. Even this becomes a delicate matter, as Mr. Justice Jackson made clear in his dissenting opinion.[42]

In what contexts, then, may a court face the question of defining what religious belief is? One question often raised is whether freedom of religious belief includes not only belief but nonbelief as well. Does religious freedom embrace the freedom of the agnostic and the atheist as well as those who have convictions about ultimate sources of values that transcend empirical observation? It seems to me that this is a question that need not be debated at length. It is not stretching the term religious liberty too far if we say that it ought to protect the freedom of those who reject religious faith as well as the freedom of the faithful. The purpose of religious liberty must be kept in mind: it is designed to protect the freedom of thought respecting ultimate values, and its scope would be artificially diminished if it did not include the liberty to question or reject familiar or established forms of religious belief. Moreover, since a function of religious liberty is to prevent government from impressing any particular belief upon a person, the freedom of the atheist and the agnostic must be as fully protected against governmental compulsion as is that of the believer. Furthermore, even if atheism and agnosticism were not sheltered by the concept of religious liberty, their freedom to entertain skepticism or nonbelief would be assured within the concept of intellectual liberty relied on in the *Barnette* case, and the freedom to propagate their views is guaranteed under the free speech and free press clauses.

The judicial understanding of religious belief is acutely involved when determining qualification for special legal privilege. A notable illustration arises under the provision of the Selective Service Act which authorizes an exemption from military service for persons who object to war on grounds of religious belief and training.[43] Religious belief is defined by statute to mean "an individual's belief in a relation to a Supreme Being involving duties superior to those arising from any human relation, but does not include essentially political, sociological, or philosophical views or a merely personal moral code." [44] Here Congress has defined religion in terms of theistic belief. In passing on the validity and application of this concept, the courts are squarely faced with the problem of the meaning of religion.

It is useful at this point to see what the Supreme Court has said in the relatively few cases in which it has had occasion to speak on the question. *Davis* v. *Beason,* decided in 1890, involved the validity of legislation prohibiting polygamy in federal territories.[45] Arguing that this statute violated the religious liberty of Mormons, the court said: "The term 'religion' has reference to one's views of his relations to his Creator, and to the obligations they impose of reverence for his being and character, and of obedience to his will. It is often confounded with the cultus or form of worship of a particular sect, but it is distinguishable from the latter." [46] According to this definition, the essential characteristic of religion is belief, as distinguished from worship or conduct, and religious belief means theistic belief. Such a conception of religious belief accords with general popular understanding. In a dissenting opinion in the *MacIntosh* case Mr. Chief Justice Hughes affirmed the statement of *Davis* when he said that the "essence of religion is belief in a relation to God involving duties superior to those arising from any human relation. . . . One cannot speak of religious liberty, with proper appreciation of its essential and historic significance, without assuming the existence of a belief in supreme allegiance to the will of God." [47]

But any notion that religious belief as embraced within the meaning of religious liberty is limited to theistic belief was dispelled by the Supreme Court's decision in *Torcaso* v. *Watkins,* decided in 1961.[48] The court held invalid under the free exercise clause of the First Amendment a requirement under the Maryland constitution that a notary public, as a part of his oath of office, declare his belief in the existence of God. Without inquiring as to what belief the petitioner did entertain, the court declared that the test oath invaded the area of belief and in putting Maryland on the side of "one particular sort of believer," namely, those who believe in the existence of God, thereby imposed a burden on the free exercise of the faiths of nonbelievers in violation of the free exercise clause.[49] Thus, the court, in finding that religious liberty protects the non-believer, not only repudiates theistic belief as essential to religion within the meaning of the Constitution, but equates nonbelief with religious belief. To buttress this conclusion, the court, speaking through Mr. Justice Black, dropped the famous footnote which reads: "Among religions in this country which do not teach what would generally be considered a belief in the existence of God are Buddhism, Taoism, Ethical Culture, Secular Humanism and others." [50]

It is not altogether clear why the court saw fit to document the opinion in this way. If religious liberty includes freedom from any public disability inspired by reference to religious belief, it was not essential to refer to what the court regarded as generally accepted nontheistic religions. Perhaps the court meant to indicate that a test could be imposed by reference to religious belief if defined broadly enough to include nontheistic systems. One may also inquire why the court did not rest its case on the ground that Maryland was here establishing a religion in violation of the First Amendment. In any event, the court's opinion, including the footnote, repudiates theistic belief as essential to religious belief.

Against this background we may examine the recent decision by the Court of Appeals of the Second Circuit in *United States* v. *Seeger,* a case involving a claim to exemption from military service under the statutory provisions discussed above.[51] Seeger claimed that his objections to war were founded on religious belief and training, even though he refused to declare a belief in God. The court found that Seeger had a faith founded on ethical considerations in terms of "moral responsibility to search for a way to maintain the recognition of the dignity and worth of the individual, the faith in reason, freedom and individuality, and the opportunity to improve life for which democracy stands." He was opposed to war because it is immoral, since it indiscriminately crushes human personality and destroys moral life.

The court found that Seeger's objection to war was based on religious training and belief even though he refused to acknowledge a theistic belief. It declared unconstitutional the statutory definition which required theistic belief, since this involved a discrimination against the holders of sincere nontheistic beliefs. Understandably, the court cited the *Torcaso* case in support of its conclusions. In equating the dictates of conscience or the imperatives of an absolute morality with religious belief for the purpose of the statutory exemption, the court adopted the statement of Judge Augustus Hand of the Second Circuit in *United States* v. *Kauten,* decided in 1943:

Religious belief arises from a sense of the inadequacy of reason as a means of relating the individual to his fellow-men and to his universe—a sense common to man in the most primitive and in the most highly civilized societies. It accepts the aid of logic but refuses to be limited by it. It is a belief finding expression in a conscience which categorically requires the believer to disregard elementary self-interest and to accept martyrdom in preference to transgressing its tenets.[52]

The *Torcaso* footnote and the *Seeger* opinion then support the view that belief in a system of ultimate moral values that bind the conscience is a form of religious belief within the meaning of the Constitution and that the grant of a statutory exemption designed to implement religious liberty must be broad enough to include such belief. But this conclusion raises important questions under the establishment clause, particularly with respect to public education. Much is said these days about the necessity of teaching moral values in the public schools. Admittedly the state has a valid secular purpose in promoting moral conduct, and admittedly many people adhere to moral values unrelated to belief in God. But if the schools consciously engage in a program of indoctrination in ethical values, resting on humanistic considerations, are they thereby contributing to the promotion and establishment of religion in the public schools? Is loyalty to ethical values a religion within the meaning of the free exercise clause but not within the meaning of the establishment clause? Does religion have different meanings under the two clauses of the First Amendment? Or does a system of ethical values assume religious significance only when it attempts to explain the source of these values and of the duty to respect them as norms of behavior? May the state then teach ethics without making this a religious teaching? These questions will receive further treatment in the fourth chapter.

A final point respecting the definition of religion is suggested by the *Torcaso* footnote, which identifies secular humanism as a form of nontheistic religion. This raises questions even more perplexing. What makes secular humanism a religion? Is it because it is an ideology or system of belief that attempts to furnish a rationale of life? But if any ideology, creed, or philosophy respecting man and society is a religion, then must not democracy, fascism, and communism also qualify as religions? It is not uncommon to refer to these as secular or quasi religions, for some find in these systems an adequate explanation of the meaning and purpose of life and the source of values that command faith and devotion. Certainly in the case of communism, with its discipline, its cultus, its sense of community, and its obligation to duties owing to the system, the resemblance to religion in the conventional sense is clearly apparent. But whether the Supreme Court would hold the Communist's faith to be protected under the free exercise clause of the First Amendment appears to be purely academic. Belief in communism or any other ideology as a way of life is privileged under the Constitution whether treated as religious belief or not. Likewise, the propagation of any political, economic, or social ideology is protected under the free speech and free press guarantees so long as it does not amount to advocacy of illegal conduct.

The reference in *Torcaso* opens up another important question respecting religious liberty. If secular humanism is a religion, then the government cannot promote it in its public institutions without violating the establishment clause. Moreover, according to the *Barnette* case, it is beyond the government's competence to prescribe or force belief in any system of thought—religious, political, or economic. Indeed, for government to throw its weight behind a secular philosophy is itself a threat to religious liberty. Recent decisions have made clear that government cannot prescribe religious teaching or practices in the public schools.[53] But it is argued that if government must ignore religion in the schools, it is by its own default promoting a secularistic philosophy, which is forbidden by the First Amendment.[54] Clearly, government cannot teach atheism, agnosticism, or secularism as a way of life. Yet government must be secular, and so must the public schools. It does not follow that merely because the schools are secular and the training is directed to secular ends, the government therefore is establishing secularism as the official creed or religion. The distinction, however, between pursuit of a secular function in which government is neutral on religion and the promotion by default of a secularistic philosophy is one that calls for tightrope walking by the government and its institutions, particularly the public schools. It is for this reason that there is properly a concern that the schools give recognition to religion in their study programs—a matter discussed in the fourth chapter.

It has been suggested that religion within the meaning of the First Amendment be defined to include the following elements: (1) a group or activity claiming to be "religious"; (2) an activity shared with a collectivity, that is, having both continuity with the past and communality in the present; (3) this collectivity engages in common cultic behavior (ritual or ethical); (4) there is a more or less coherent or common creed or body of beliefs which the members profess, though some or all of the concepts therein may be held by nonreligious persons.[55] This definition clearly embraces religion in the conventional sense, but it introduces a number of difficulties. Any so-called secular ideology shared by a group would fit within it, provided that the adherents claimed that they were a "religious" group or were engaged in a "religious" activity. One may also seriously question whether religion in the constitutional sense must be identified with a collectivity or a corporate body such as a church. Seeger's conscientious conviction about war was held to be a religion even though not shared with a defined collectivity. The nondenominational prayer held invalid in *Engel* as a religious exercise was not identified with any particular collectivity, unless the collectivity could be defined in terms of the civil community that sanctioned this practice.

It is too much to expect that the courts will ever frame a comprehensive definition of religion adequate for all purposes under the First Amendment. Yet they do face the job of giving meaning to the terms used in concrete problems that come before them. The real difficulty is that any meaningful definition of religion must in the end take account of the theological significance of the term. The Court of Appeals for the Second Circuit in the *Jakobson* case held that belief in "Godness" was equivalent to belief in God for purpose of claiming exemption under the Universal Military Training and Service Act.[56] If referred to the writings of Bishop John A. T. Robinson and Professor Paul Tillich in support of the view that belief in God need not be limited to belief in a Supreme Being or to a

conception that attributes certain qualities to God. It may well
be that the opinion in the *Jakobson* case opens the way to a
constitutional definition of religion that transcends traditional
theism and recognizes a wide variety of religious belief, yet
avoids the implication of *Torcaso* that any secular ideology
must be characterized as religion under the First Amendment.
Certainly the *Torcaso* decision and its footnote leave the matter
in an unsatisfactory state. It is not inappropriate to suggest that
theologians have a contribution to make in dealing with this
question and that the Supreme Court would be well advised
to turn to them for such assistance as they can give.

Turning to the Supreme Court's decisions defining the scope
of religious liberty, we find ourselves on much more solid
ground. In a number of decisions—dealing for the most part
with Jehovah's Witnesses—the court has mapped out a broad
field for the free exercise of religion. Many issues are now
clearly settled. In the name of religious liberty persons can
claim freedom from coercion of conscience, freedom from the
imposition of any official religious belief, freedom of worship,
freedom from any compulsion to support religious activities
through taxes, freedom to make their faith manifest and to
seek converts through proselytization, freedom to assemble
as a congregation, freedom to witness to their faith in many
ways, and freedom to solicit for religious purposes.[57] I emphasize these particular categories since they go to the heart
of religious liberty as it reflects individual freedom. In the
constitutions of some foreign countries a distinction is made
between religious liberty as a facet of individual freedom and
the freedoms that may be claimed by religious bodies in their
corporate capacities.[58] In the United States we have not so
clearly distinguished between the religious freedom of individuals and the corporate freedoms that church bodies may
exercise. Our courts treat the right of persons to organize and

operate congregations and the right of churches to carry on their collective activities as integral parts of religious liberty.[59] Under the laws of most states religious bodies are given freedom to incorporate and to enjoy the advantages of corporate status. It is interesting, though, to observe that in the constitutions of Virginia[60] and West Virginia[61] the privilege of incorporation is expressly denied to churches. Such a limitation suggests (particularly since it originated in the state where Jefferson and Madison had much influence) that religious freedom is considered a personal matter and that it does not necessarily extend to some corporate privileges including the freedom to incorporate.

On the other hand, the freedom to carry on as an organization includes the freedom to acquire and own property and to enter into contracts. This, however, is not a distinctive aspect of religious freedom but is a freedom that churches as nonprofit corporations and juridical personalities may enjoy as do other legal personalities. The freedom to engage in eleemosynary activities, such as schools, colleges, and welfare enterprises, is regarded by the churches as a proper expression of their religious concern and an important element of their constitutional freedom, although this is not expressly recognized in constitutions and may be viewed as part of a broader freedom of voluntaristic nonprofit enterprise.

Similarly, the freedom of churches to publish religious books and materials may be categorized in terms either of religious liberty or of freedom of the press. The freedom of churches acting in corporate capacities through their councils, congregations, and national church bodies to witness for the church on matters of public concern is peculiarly identifiable with their religious witness and is an important aspect of religious liberty, even though it is also identifiable with free speech and free press. Finally, mention should be made of the freedom enjoyed by the churches in managing their religious affairs and administering their spiritual discipline in accordance with their own internal law and procedure, free from intervention by the legislatures or by the civil courts. The Supreme Court has made clear that churches can claim this immunity in the name of religious liberty.[62] This immunity emerges as a fundamental aspect of the separation principle.

Any consideration of the dimensions of religious liberty must also take account of possible limitations which may be imposed upon it by law. A thorough discussion of permissible limitations would furnish the subject of a separate volume. But some fundamental considerations should be noted. In the first place, the concept of religious liberty, as pointed out earlier in this chapter, should include freedom from discrimination on religious grounds in the enjoyment of legal rights, privileges, and immunities. This principle can be stated in equal protection terms, but it can also be viewed as an application of the principle of religious liberty. If a city makes its parks available for assemblies generally but denies them to persons meeting for religious purposes, this discrimination may be viewed either as an impairment of religious liberty or as a violation of the equal protection clause. If a city provides that all children of school age are eligible to receive certain free medical and dental treatment except children attending parochial schools, this again is discrimination based on religious grounds in the enjoyment of common privilege.

Yet the principle that the religious factor cannot furnish the basis for discriminatory treatment is not completely unqualified. As noted earlier, state constitutions commonly prohibit the use of public funds to aid sectarian schools or religious institutions or corporations. Here a policy of discrimination in the use of public funds is given express constitutional sanction. If the public policy of the state is to limit the use of educational funds to schools under public control, this involves no discrimination except the distinction between schools under public and those under private control—a distinction well recognized in our law. But if public funds are made available for all educational institutions whether public or private except those that are under the control of a religious body, it is indeed hard to avoid the conclusion that the religious factor is being used as a ground for disqualification from public benefits. It is significant that there is no sanction in our law for discrimination against an individual because of his religious belief. Discriminations based upon the religious factor have to do with activities in which the churches engage in a corporate capacity, such as the operation of schools, hospitals, and related types of institutions. These historically sanctioned discriminations must find their justification in those basic conceptions of public policy that underlie the principle of separation of church and state—whether it be the desirability of maintaining the voluntaristic character of church enterprises, the importance of protecting government against ecclesiastical demands and aggrandizement, or apprehension of disruptive social consequences that may flow from use of public funds to support church-related educational programs. Any statement of these considerations anticipates the problems discussed in the following chapters. The point I wish to emphasize here is that the general principle of freedom from discriminatory classification on the basis of religion has not been fully recognized in American law.

Apart from the principle of nondiscrimination, religious liberty has its own substantive content, as recognized by the Supreme Court. The chief question respecting permissible limitations on religious liberty concerns those general regulatory laws which do not discriminate in their application on the basis of religious belief and activity. In short, can religious liberty be asserted as a ground for claiming immunity to laws of general operation? Two types of general laws may be considered: (1) those which are designed to promote the public health, safety, morals, and general welfare in the exercise of the state's police power and which do not directly limit or restrict the free expression of ideas; and (2) those which are directed against various forms of expression of ideas and which are justified on the ground of protecting the public peace and internal security.

The laws falling into the first category present the least difficulty—where limitations on religious liberty are concerned —so long as these laws meet the general test of reasonableness. When religious belief becomes manifest in overt conduct, it is subject to limitations imposed in the interest of public order, which includes the health, safety, morals, and general welfare of the community.[63] Thus, laws may require medical treatment to minimize the spread of contagious disease, even though it may offend religious belief.[64] They may prohibit conduct that disturbs the public peace,[65] require parents to observe child labor laws when using children to propagandize religious views,[66] prohibit practices such as polygamy which offend the community's sense of morals,[67] and subject churches to restrictions imposed by planning and zoning laws.[68] This is not to suggest that such laws are necessarily valid in their application to a given situation, but that religious liberty furnishes no ground for claiming immunity to laws which place reasonable restrictions on overt conduct in the furtherance of public interests protected by the state's police power. Here the restriction on religious liberty is indirect.

The second category of general laws, namely, those that directly abridge or restrict the free expression of ideas in the interest of public peace and security, creates more difficulty. The expression of religious ideas is closely identified with freedom of speech, press, and assembly, and whether in literature, in the pulpit, or in proselytizing activities should receive no less protection than other forms of free speech. It is not enough to say that religious freedom, along with the general freedoms of speech and press, is subject to laws enacted to advance the common good. Although it is generally recognized that individual liberties are subject to the reasonable exercise of the police power, the freedoms of expression protected under the First Amendment have been said by the Supreme Court to be preferred freedoms which cannot be directly limited or abridged by public authority except in cases warranted by clear and present danger of public evils.[69] In other words, there must be strong and compelling public interests to warrant a restriction on religious freedom and on the related freedoms of speech and press. Though the status of the clear-and-present-danger rule is now somewhat in doubt, it is clear from the cases that the Supreme Court does continue to give a preferred treatment to freedom of expression by invalidating statutes and ordinances that restrict First Amendment freedoms in the absence of clear and compelling reasons in support of the restrictions. In a series of decisions upholding the right of Jehovah's Witnesses to engage in proselytizing activities of various kinds and to use public parks for religious services, the Supreme Court has attempted to maintain religious liberty at a high level of constitutional protection. Some of these cases have rested on the ground of religious liberty; others have rested on the free speech and free press guarantees. In any event, it is fair to say that the court has shown special astuteness in protecting the freedom of religious expression.[70]

Earlier in this chapter I pointed out that the religious factor has been used as the basis for preferred treatment in the enjoyment of certain rights, privileges, and immunities: tax exemptions for houses of worship and for religious activities by religious corporations,[71] immunities granted churches and religious activities under tax and general police laws such as wage and hour laws,[72] exemptions from military service[73] and from Sunday closing laws on religious grounds.[74] In some instances churches enjoy exemptions along with other nonprofit voluntaristic associations, so that this is not a special case of privilege or exemption on distinctively religious grounds, but rather a case where the churches and religious activities fit into a broader classification.

Perhaps even more striking are the Supreme Court decisions invalidating statutes and ordinances on the ground that they restricted religious liberty.[75] These decisions, as suggested above, give religious liberty the benefit not only of the judicial protection accorded the First Amendment generally, but they recognize it as an independent liberty and give it a special and preferred position.

Local ordinances imposing license taxes on the sale of books and other literature and imposing special restrictions on house-to-house canvassing and solicitation have been declared invalid in their application to Jehovah's Witnesses.[76] In other words, the Supreme Court requires, at least in some instances, that special exemptions be granted on religious grounds from regulatory and tax laws of general application.

It is understandable, for reasons stated at the beginning of this chapter, why religious liberty should be treated as an independent substantive liberty and why because of the nature of this liberty it may receive favored treatment from the legislature by means of exemptions granted on religious grounds from laws of general operation. It is also understandable why the court may hold that regard for religious liberty requires an exemption from regulatory and tax laws where these laws operate as a direct restraint on religious activity, even though they do not discriminate against these activities; or why the court may apply a stricter standard in judging the validity of general laws as they apply to restrain the free expression of religious ideas. But once it is recognized that religious liberty occupies a preferred position, it is difficult to determine when general laws operate as an invalid restraint on the free exercise of religion. More specifically, does the status of religious liberty as a preferred freedom require the invalidation of laws of general operation insofar as they result in some indirect burden on religious liberty?

In dealing with this question we turn to two cases which present strikingly parallel problems. In the *Braunfeld* case the court, with three justices dissenting, held that a state in enacting a Sunday closing law was not required to grant a special exemption for those persons who because of religious conviction observe a day other than Sunday as a day of rest.[77] While indicating that such an exemption might be permitted, the court stated that it was not required and pointed to practical considerations that a state might consider in deciding that such an exemption would not be feasible or desirable. The statute was directed to appropriate secular ends within the scope of the state's police power, did not discriminate on religious grounds, did not in its application operate as a direct restraint on religious activity, but did operate as an indirect burden on religious liberty. The case seemed to fit squarely into the proposition advanced above that a constitutional immunity may not be claimed on religious grounds to general laws enacted in the reasonable exercise of the police power to advance appropriate public interests where the impact on religious liberty is indirect or incidental. But then in the later *Sherbert* case the court held that the free exercise clause required a state to give a special exemption to Seventh-Day Adventists in administering unemployment compensation laws.[78] Benefits under this law could not be refused because the petitioner had refused on religious grounds to take a job for which she was qualified but which required her to work on Saturday. The case might have rested on the narrower ground of discrimination since the South Carolina law did accord a privileged position to persons who refused on religious grounds to work on Sunday, but the court chose to rest its case on the broad ground of the free exercise clause. Mr. Justice Brennan, speaking for the majority, stated that the Seventh-Day Adventist should not have to choose between following her faith and getting the benefit of the state's unemployment compensation laws. Here is a case where a state law of general operation was held invalid because it imposed an indirect burden on religious liberty. Three justices thought that the decision had the effect of overruling the *Braunfeld* case. But the majority opinion distinguished *Braunfeld* on the ground that the same practical considerations and difficulties arising from the granting of Sunday closing law exemptions were not relevant in this situation. The court undertook its own scrutiny of any difficulties that might arise in granting a favored position on religious grounds in the administration of an unemployment compensation law. In substance, the court engaged in a balancing process and decided that there were not sufficiently weighty considerations of public policy to warrant this indirect impingement on religious liberty. It is hardly necessary to say that *Sherbert* extends in a significant way the constitutional protection accorded religious liberty.

General laws are invalid insofar as they impose indirect burdens on the free exercise of religion unless there is some compelling state interest which justifies this infringement on religious liberty. The court applied a more stringent test than it has usually applied when indirect encroachments upon First Amendment freedoms are involved. *Sherbert* opens up new vistas on religious liberty and suggests a reconsideration of results reached in some earlier cases. Whether religious liberty should be carried so far in creating exemptions to laws of general application is questionable. In *Braunfeld* the court stated persuasive reasons why exemptions on religious grounds should not be required where general statutes operate indirectly to place an economic burden on the free exercise of religion. The distinction made in *Sherbert* is not very convincing. But whatever else may be said of *Sherbert*, it does affirm the conclusion that religious liberty is recognized as an independent liberty, that it occupies a preferred position, and that the court will not permit encroachments upon this liberty, whether direct or indirect, unless required by clear and compelling considerations of public policy. It also makes clear that no definite rules can be prescribed respecting permissible restrictions on religious liberty and that the court arrives at a decision by the pragmatic process of examining the burdens placed on that liberty and the nature and importance of the countervailing public interests that are advanced to justify the restriction. The appraisal and balancing of these conflicting interests is a function of the judicial process, and the end result is a matter of subjective judgment.

Religious liberty, including the freedom of the individual and the freedom of the churches, has wide dimensions and enjoys an exalted place in our constitutional order. It embraces not only freedom of belief but a wide variety of activities essential to the expression of religious faith and commitment. The Supreme Court has made a notable contribution in its decisions which have elevated religious liberty to the position of a preferred freedom, not only because religious activities cannot be abridged except for clear and compelling reasons related to the public interest, but also because in some situations the legislature may, and in other situations must, take the religious factor into account as a basis for preferential treatment under tax and regulatory laws. In short, the duty to respect religious liberty carries with it the power to implement this liberty by special legislative measures and even the duty to accommodate legislation to religious conviction as long as countervailing policy considerations are not clearly demonstrable. But to say that government may or must grant a preferred position to religion at once suggests further problems under the establishment clause of the First Amendment. How far may or must government use its power to aid the free exercise of religion without violating the competing constitutional principle that it may not pass laws respecting an establishment of religion? We turn to these questions in the next chapter.

3

THE FIRST AMENDMENT:

Dilemma of Interpretation

The First Amendment states that Congress shall make no law respecting an establishment of religion or prohibiting the free exercise thereof. These twin phrases create the dilemma which is the subject of this chapter.

The free exercise clause operates as a direct restriction on Congress and by judicial construction carries over through the due process clause of the Fourteenth Amendment as a restriction on the states. Its general purpose is to assure religious liberty a protected place in our constitutional order. The questions that arise under it concern the dimensions of this liberty as an independent substantive freedom and the limitations that may be imposed upon it. In turning our attention to the interpretation of the establishment limitation, it is important to keep in mind the considerations respecting religious liberty as they arise under the free exercise clause. The problems of establishment under the First Amendment cannot be considered in isolation from the central concept of religious liberty.

It is not possible in the course of this chapter to deal exhaustively with the historical background and original purpose, if indeed one may be found, of the establishment language of the First Amendment. Some considerations, however, may be mentioned briefly. In the first place, a principal historical purpose underlying the establishment clause was to state a jurisdictional limitation on Congress by denying it power to interfere with state religious establishments. It made clear that this was not a subject within the competence of the federal government. Whether or not the original purpose of insuring the states' freedom to control religious establishments has been achieved is a matter that will receive further attention later. But the language is not clearly stated as merely a limitation on the power of Congress to interfere with state religious establishments. It is a direct and substantive limitation on the power of Congress, though couched in ambiguous terms that admit of various interpretations, so that the apparent historical purpose of keeping the federal government from encroaching upon the control of the states over their established churches, while useful and relevant in furnishing a clue to the meaning of the establishment language, does not furnish a compelling answer to the question: What is a law respecting an establishment of religion?

A natural construction of this language suggests that what is prohibited is a law respecting a religious establishment—a term that has reference to a church—and that the purpose is to prevent Congressional laws dealing directly with ecclesiastical matters, whether it be a law establishing a national church in the conventional sense, sanctioning the creed of a particular church, asserting control over churches and their officers, or contributing funds in direct aid of churches or levying taxes in their direct support. The history of establishment in England and in the colonies as well as in the states following the Revolutionary War supports this conclusion. But the language may also be construed to forbid laws that establish religion, in which case the verbal aspect of the term establishment is emphasized.

The search for original meaning and historical purpose underlying this language has yielded inconclusive results, and it would not be profitable to explore this matter in detail. In the end the Supreme Court is free to give this language the meaning it chooses, whether guided by the court's interpretation of historical purpose or by the court's use of this ambiguous language in accommodating constitutional interpretation to the felt needs of the day. But some considerations are worth noting. The court has attached great significance to the views of Madison and Jefferson in defining the general historical purpose of the religion clauses of the First Amendment and in fixing the meaning of the establishment limitation. This is understandable. Madison played a leading part in the historic struggle against the proposal before the Virginia legislature to levy taxes for the support of teachers of religion. The Memorial and Remonstrance which he drafted remains a classic statement in support of the separation of church and state. The state, he argued, as secular authority has jurisdiction over temporal matters. This jurisdiction does not extend to spiritual matters, which are the domain of private belief and the churches. The churches sacrifice their spiritual independence if they look to government to achieve their purposes. When government meddles in religious matters, it invites competition by the churches in seeking favors and the risk of ecclesiastical domination with all the dangers of persecuting dissenters and coercing belief. Madison thus took a strong stand against governmental involvement in religious affairs. In this he was seconded by Thomas Jefferson, who drafted the Virginia Bill for Religious Liberty. Jefferson shared Madison's views that the temporal authority had no jurisdiction over religious matters. By the covenant of government the people had reserved matters of belief to themselves and had excluded it from the province of their government. Interpreting the First Amendment to correspond to his own views, he wrote in his letter to the Danbury Baptists that the effect of this amendment was to establish "a wall of separation between church and state." [1]

Madison and Jefferson, children of the Enlightenment, represented the secular and humanistic view that supported religious liberty and the separation of church and state. For them the separation principle was indispensable to the freedom of belief, conscience, and dissent that are threatened when government intrudes in religious matters or when ecclesiastical authorities use government to advance their ends. They were as much concerned with freedom *from* religion as with freedom *of* religion. Their concern reflected the struggle in Virginia over the assessment of taxes to support teachers of religion during the colonial era when the established church was taken for granted. This point furnishes evidence that Madison and Jefferson were concerned with governmental laws and practices which dealt directly and distinctly with religious and ecclesiastical matters. Their views did not stem from hostility to religion, which they considered a private and voluntary matter: they were concerned about keeping religion out of the domain of public affairs.

That Madison and Jefferson contributed much to the American experiment in religious liberty and the separation of church and state is indisputable. But credit must also be given to Roger Williams and other religious leaders who (reflecting the Anabaptist tradition) saw religious liberty and freedom from state control as indispensable to the full freedom of the Christian faith, which must rest on voluntarism and the working of the Spirit. Certainly religious, as well as secular, considerations shaped the ideas behind the separation principle. Finally, there was the very practical consideration that, given the diversity of sects and the emerging religious pluralism, no one church could expect to maintain its position as the established church or the officially preferred religion.

Conceding the part played by Madison and Jefferson in the struggle to establish the separation principle, one may ask how conclusive their views were in the interpretation of the First Amendment and partciularly of the establishment clause. That the Supreme Court has attached great importance to them is clear. Madison played a leading role in the Congressional committee that drafted the First Amendment. Indeed, Mr. Justice Black has referred to him as the author of the First Amendment.[2] Irving Brant, Madison's biographer, credits him with the leading role in drafting the religion clauses.[3] But the Reverend Anson Phelps Stokes, eminent historian of church-state relations in the United States, presents evidence that the language adopted in the final draft was composed by Samuel Livermore.[4] It seems relevant, therefore, to ask what was the goal of the committee that approved the First Amendment. Yet the studies for the committee proceedings leave the matter in doubt as to whether the language chosen was to prohibit laws giving preference to one or more religious establishments, or to prohibit Congress from passing laws which placed the power or support of government behind any or all ecclesiatsical establishments and religious practices. Moreover, a constitutional amendment which is approved by Congress and ratified by the states cannot be construed on the basis of any one person unless his interpretation is so well known, so clearly expressed, and so generally accepted that it could be understood to have conveyed the sense of the ratifying authorities. There is little evidence to document any consensus on the meaning of the establishment limitation.

All this suggests the difficulties in using Madison and Jeffer-

son as authoritative interpreters of the establishment language
of the First Amendment. Even if their views are accepted
as authoritative, the application of their views to contemporary problems points to no conclusive answer. Madison and
Jefferson were speaking from the experience of direct governmental support of ecclesiastical establishments and officers. A
strict separation theory and a wall of separation metaphor were
therefore relevant.

What Madison may have thought about the implications of
the separation principle for the whole interrelationship of law
and religion is by no means clear. Nor do his views shed light
on the question of whether government may give aid or support
to any religious activity which is incidental to a general program. The same is true of Thomas Jefferson, who seemed to
recognize the value of religion in society and, indeed, envisioned
in some cases a cooperative arrangement between government
and churches which did not involve use of the state's coercive
power in forcing religious belief on citizens. As stated by Mr.
Justice Brennan in his concurring opinion in the *Schempp* case
decided in 1963, it is futile to look to Jefferson and Madison
for answers to contemporary problems, but the views they entertained are relevant in determing the evils contemplated from
a concert of church and state and the values to be served by
the constitutional limitation.[5]

For present-day problems it is more useful to look at what
the Supreme Court has said in construing this language and
what actual results have been reached in its application. It is
also useful to keep in mind that when the Supreme Court for
the first time in recent years began to concern itself with the
meaning of the establishment language, the nation had behind
it a fairly long history following the adoption of the First
Amendment and following the adoption of many state constitutions, which employed more precise language in dealing with

questions of this nature. Attention was called in the second chapter to the provisions commonly found in state constitutions which not only recognize freedom of belief and worship but which also provide that no one shall be compelled to pay taxes in support of a house of worship or of a teacher of religion and that no public monies shall be used for the support of sectarian education or in aid of religious corporations.[6]

These provisions reflect at least in part the struggles that were culminating when the First Amendment was adopted. They have considerable value, for they state more precisely what may have been intended by the broad establishment language of the First Amendment: they indicate that a state should not use its coercive powers, including the power of taxation, to compel acceptance of religious belief or to support ecclesiastical institutions and their ministers. The state constitutions embody the tradition that not only do citizens have the right to the free exercise of religion, but government cannot compel belief or force financial contributions in distinctive support of ecclesiastical institutions and officers and of religious practices.

Historical practices sanctioned by many years of usage should also be noted. Support of the military chaplaincy by the early Congresses, consisting in part of men who had a voice in drafting and approving the First Amendment, suggests that they thought the establishment clause did not preclude governmental support of this particular kind of religious activity. For the better part of two centuries state constitutions have in various forms provided for tax exemptions of property used for houses of worship or for religious purposes.[7] Here again is a practical construction, authenticated by history, of the meaning of the separation principle in American life. The American constitutional tradition has thus accepted a distinction between direct governmental support of churches and the indirect assistance furnished by tax exemptions. This may not be a logical distinction, but as Mr. Justice Holmes observed, "a page of history is worth a volume of logic." [8] It was also Mr. Justice Holmes who said that the purpose of the Fourteenth Amendment was not to undo two hundred years of history, and this aphorism may be applied to some of the questions that have been raised about the validity of long-sanctioned practices.[9] If, as Mr. Justice Frankfurter said in his separate opinion in the McCollum case, the principle of separation was well accepted at the time of the Fourteenth Amendment and should therefore enter into the interpretation of the due process clause of the same amendment, then the practice of separation as known in 1868 should furnish an illuminating commentary on its meaning in American life.[10] The Supreme Court's interpretations make clear that the sanction of history does not necessarily validate practices in the current setting of constitutional interpretations, and it is fair to say that the court is now interpreting the establishment limitation to conform to its understanding of the separation principle in the light of the new religious pluralism. But the simple point remains that to the extent that the court relies on history to authenticate its interpretations, it does well to look at the total historical development and not simply to pick and choose the elements of history that it finds useful to bolster its current interpretations.

As for interpretations of the establishment language by the Supreme Court, one is struck by the paucity of decisions in this area. Whereas the interpretation of the free exercise clause has given rise to a substantial body of decisions, only a handful of decisions—most of them of very recent vintage—are available on the interpretation of the establishment language. Although the question was raised before the Supreme Court in 1899 in a case involving Congressional appropriations for a hospital operated by Catholic sisters in the District of Columbia,[11] it was not until 1947, in the famous Everson case, that the Court attempted to give a broad comprehensive meaning to this language and had recourse to history in order to authenticate this meaning.[12] One reason for the limited number of decisions in this area is that it is extremely difficult for any person to acquire proper standing to raise a First Amendment issue which turns on the use of funds in support of religious institutions or practices. The doctrine of the *Frothingham* case that a taxpayer as such does not have standing to raise questions about federal spending stands in the way of litigation challenging various federal practices.[13] A second consideration is that many of the states have provisions specifically directed against the use of governmental funds for particular religious activities.[14] These have furnished a substantial protection against state involvement in religious matters. A third consideration is that the judicial action in making the First Amendment apply to the states via the Fourteenth Amendment is a recent development. Indeed, the first extended exploration of the establishment clause as a limitation on the states occurred in the *Everson* case, decided in 1947.

Before we turn to an examination of the theories advanced by the Supreme Court in the interpretation of the establishment language, it will be useful to give a brief account of the decisions in which the establishment clause has played a part. These can be stated in short order. In the *Everson* case the Supreme Court held that the use of public funds to reimburse parents for the cost of sending children to schools was not unconstitutional to the extent that these funds were also made available to children going to parochial schools. The court found that the law authorizing this kind of assistance, which at least indirectly gave aid to parochial school education, was not a law respecting an establishment of religion. Four justices dissented. Later, in the *McCollum* case, with only Mr. Justice Reed dissenting, the court for the first time relied on the establishment clause to invalidate a state practice.[15] It held that a public school program whereby children were released for one hour from the regular public school program to attend religious instruction given on the school premises by teachers supplied by the religious communities was a use of the state's coercive power in aid of religious instruction and a violation of the establishment limitation. Yet not long after that the court held in the *Zorach* case that where released time was conducted off the school premises, no violation of the establishment clause resulted.[16] Four justices dissenting thought that the case was governed by the *McCollum* decision. Then came the decision in the Sunday closing cases that a state law requiring cessation of business activities on Sunday was not a law establishing the Christian religion since the law was designed to achieve a secular purpose.[17] Mr. Justice Douglas dissented. The cases dealing with prayer and Bible-reading in the public schools are the latest in this series. In its decisions in the *Engel* [18] and the *Schempp* [19] cases, with Mr. Justice Stewart dissenting, the court held that state laws or actions of local school boards requiring the recitation of prayers, whether sectarian or not, and the reading without comment of the Bible as part of a public school program violated the establishment limitation.

The upshot of all this is that there are six important decisions of modern vintage interpreting the establishment clause. In three of these cases, namely, those involving bus transportation for parochial school children, Sunday closing, and released time off the school premises, the court found no violation of the establishment limitation. Violations were found in the case involving released time on school premises and in the two cases dealing with prayer and Bible-reading exercises in public schools. The opinions in these cases furnish grist for our further study in determining what theory or theories the court has elaborated in its interpretation of the establishment clause.

First, however, there are two questions of considerable importance in these cases which do not turn on the substantive meaning of the establishment clause. All of these cases involve the effect on the states of the First Amendment limitation, which states that Congress shall make no law respecting an establishment of religion. Although we cannot here explore at length questions on the use of the Fourteenth Amendment as a vehicle for making the First Amendment apply to the states, we might note that the Supreme Court has up to now rejected the thesis advanced by some justices that the purpose of the Fourteenth Amendment was to make the entire Bill of Rights apply to the states.[20] On the contrary, the court has in general adhered to the theory that only the fundamental rights of persons are protected against state abridgement through the due process clause of the Fourteenth Amendment.[21] In application of this theory the court has said that the fundamental freedoms of the First Amendment are incorporated in the phrasing of the due process clause of the Fourteenth Amendment and thus become limitations on state power.

In a short-cut application of this idea (and this is the way the law develops) the court has said in numerous opinions that the First Amendment is applicable to the states.[22] It was easily understandable that the religious liberty secured by the free exercise clause would be regarded as a fundamental right protected by the Fourteenth Amendment. But by a blanket application of the First Amendment to the states the court could then say in the *Everson* case that the establishment limitation was also applicable to the states. The court has shown no disposition to question this conclusion in recent cases, although it still remains for the court to demonstrate in what respect a person is deprived of life, liberty, or property without due process of law because of the violation of the establishment limitation. Mr. Justice Stewart recognized the problem when he stated in his dissenting opinion in *Schempp* that the establishment clause was "somehow" incorporated into the due process clause of the Fourteenth Amendment, but he did not offer any explanation or discuss the implications of dealing with it as a due process problem.[23] It may be, as Mr. Justice Frankfurter suggested in his separate opinion in *McCollum*, that the principle of separation of church and state had become a nationally accepted principle at the time the Fourteenth Amendment was adopted and is therefore one of those institutions fundamental to our conceptions of liberty and justice which the due process clause protects against state impairment.[24]

In his separate opinion in *Schempp* Mr. Justice Brennan took the bull by the horns and stated that freedom from a law respecting an establishment of religion could be regarded as a fundamental right for the purpose of the due process clause.[25] But Mr. Justice Brennan's solution oversimplifies the problem. The Fourteenth Amendment states that no person shall be deprived of life, liberty, or property without due process of law. It protects against invasion of personal rights and serves as a jurisdictional limitation on governmental power only to prevent deprivation of life, liberty, or property without due process. It should follow, then, that a violation of the establishment limitation raises a due process question only if it has the effect of depriving a person of liberty or property, and this without due process of law. Such a deprivation may be seen to occur if a state subjects a person to coercive practices that impair freedom of belief or conscience or force him to pay taxes to support a governmentally sanctioned religion. Yet the opinions in *Engel* and *Schempp* were not based on the ground that the prayer and Bible-reading exercises violated personal or property rights. Moreover, the court's general position has been that a deprivation of a right protected by the

Fourteenth Amendment is consistent with due process if it results from a reasonable exercise of the states' power in promoting certain public objectives.

This might suggest a tempering of the establishment limitation when employed in the due process context. Yet there is no hint in the recent cases that the concept of reasonableness in balancing public interest against invasion of private right was a relevant consideration. It is a striking fact that the court has abandoned familiar due process considerations in making the establishment limitation applicable to the states, even though the due process clause furnishes the vehicle for relating this limitation to state action. It is understandable that Mr. Justice Clark should have said in his *Schempp* opinion that this question is now academic, since his reliance on the court's earlier *ipse dixits* and holdings spared him the difficulty of explaining how an amendment directed to Congress is now made applicable to the states without reference to the due process considerations that are relevant in invoking the Fourteenth Amendment.[26] One can hardly avoid the conclusion that the Supreme Court is using the due process clause as a convenient tool to impose upon the states a conception of national policy which it regards as peculiarly appropriate to present conditions. Because of differences in the religious make-up of communities throughout the country, it is not clear that it is either desirable or feasible to enforce a national policy on such matters as prayer and Bible-reading exercises in the public schools, except where necessary to prevent a substantial invasion of personal liberty. But the Supreme Court has spoken, and the results of these cases supply further evidence of the freedom and boldness with which the court has at various stages of our history used the Fourteenth Amendment as a vehicle for fastening basic policy limitations upon the states.

The second collateral question is that of the standing needed to raise questions under the establishment clause. The standing problem raises the vital question of whether it is necessary to show a violation of personal right or freedom as the result of alleged violation of the establishment limitation. If a person claims that his personal freedom is impaired in some substantial way by a program sanctioning or supporting religious practices, no question of standing is raised. Indeed, the question can easily be resolved under the free exercise rather than the establishment clause. Or if a person contends that as a taxpayer he is asked to pay taxes levied to support governmentally sanctioned religious practices, he ought to have standing as a taxpayer. But as I have previously pointed out, a federal taxpayer has no standing as such to question the spending of federal monies.[27] On the other hand, local taxpayers have standing to challenge state and local spending alleged to violate federal constitutional limitations, provided they can show out-of-pocket costs attributable to the practices challenged as unconstitutional. Without a basis for standing as taxpayer or a claim of invasion of constitutional right, the only other possibility of raising the establishment limitation is to show that the challenged practice adversely affects some personal interest, even though it falls short of a constitutionally protected right. This was the theory followed in the recent *Schempp* case where the court stated that parents would have standing to question the validity of religious practices in public schools since they and their children were most immediately affected, even though the court expressly denied that it was resting the case on a claim of invasion of constitutional liberty.[28] But apart from dealing with the specific problem before the court, the recent cases shed no new light on the question of who has standing to raise questions arising under the establishment clause.

We return now to the opinions interpreting the establishment clause to see what light they shed on theories reflecting its meaning and application. The most extensive probing of the establishment clause appears in the cases mentioned above. An examination of them reveals three principal theories and suggests that the court is still struggling to find a rationale that relates the establishment and the free exercise clauses in a meaningful way and supplies a basis for cohesive interpretation of both clauses. These three theories may be described as follows:

1. The theory that the establishment clause viewed in conjunction with the free exercise clause requires a strict separation of church and state and that government can do nothing which involves governmental support of religion or which is favorable to the cultivation of religious interests.

2. The theory that the establishment clause requires government to be neutral with respect to religious matters and that in its legislation and programs it cannot, therefore, do anything which either aids or hinders religion.

3. The theory that any limitations derived from the establishment limitation cannot be rigidly applied so as to preclude all aid to religion or to require absolute neutrality, that questions arising under the establishment limitation cannot be viewed in isolation from the free exercise guarantee, and that in some situations government *must*, and in other situations *may*, accommodate its policies and laws in the furtherance of religious freedom.

The first two theories are essentially conceptual in character. The third represents a pragmatic approach. We now examine these theories more closely.

1. *The Strict Separation Theory*. This theory found its first and most notable expression in the famous opinion by Mr. Justice Black in the *Everson* case where it was held that the use of public funds to provide transportation for children to

parochial as well as public schools did not violate the establishment limitation. But it was in the course of this opinion that Mr. Justice Black gave a broad and comprehensive interpretation of the establishment clause—an interpretation founded on his conception of the historical purpose underlying this clause as evidenced by the views of Madison and Jefferson. The critical paragraph in his opinion reads as follows:

The "establishment of religion" clause of the First Amendment means at least this: Neither a state nor the federal government can set up a church. Neither can pass laws which aid one religion, aid all religions, or prefer one religion over another. Neither can force nor influence a person to go to or remain away from church against his will or force him to profess a belief or disbelief in any religion. No person can be punished for entertaining or professing religious beliefs or disbeliefs, for church attendance or non-church attendance. No tax in any amount, large or small, can be levied to support any religious activities or institutions, whatever they may be called, or whatever form they may adopt to teach or practice religion. Neither the state nor the federal government can, openly or secretly, participate in the affairs of any religious organizations or groups and vice versa. In the words of Jefferson, the clause against establishment of religion by law was intended to erect "a wall of separation between church and state." [29]

It is evident that many ideas are here brought together in a rather loose way and that some of them attributed to the establishment limitation are more aptly brought under the free exercise clause. This is true of the statements that no person can be punished for entertaining or professing a religion or religious beliefs or disbeliefs or for church attendance or nonattendance and that no one can force or influence a person to go to or stay away from church against his will or force him to profess his belief or disbelief in any religion. The part of the opinion, however, which says that the government cannot pass laws which aid one religion, aid all religions, or prefer one religion over another does suggest something distinctive about the meaning of establishment, as does the statement that no tax can be levied to support any religious activities or institutions, whatever they may be called or whatever form they may adopt. What seems to be the real nub of this interpretation of the establishment language, insofar as it achieves results distinguishable from the free exercise clause, is that it prohibits aid to all religions. In other words, the establishment clause embodies the principle of separation of church and state, and this principle not only prohibits an established church or the giving of preferential treatment to one or more churches but also prohibits multiple establishments as well. The key idea that emerges from *Everson* is sometimes described as the principle of "no-aid," namely, that government cannot by its programs, policies, or laws do anything to aid or support religion or religious activities. The ideas expressed and the general tone of the opinion rest on a broad construction of establishment to support strict separation, and it is fitting that in support of this construction Mr. Justice Black should have concluded by invoking Jefferson's famous wall of separation between church and state.

The decision in *McCollum*—the first released time case—was based squarely on the theory advanced in *Everson*.[30] The use of the public school system to promote religious instruction was a use of governmental power in support of religion. Much of the general absolutism of the *Everson* theory underlies the decision in the *Engel* case, which invalidated under the establishment clause a school board's regulation prescribing daily recitation of a nonsectarian prayer in public schools.[31] The *Engel* opinion did not cite the *Everson* case or, indeed, any other cases, but in falling back on basic historical considerations with respect to concert of church and state and the necessity of preventing the slightest infringement of separation, it carried forward the essential philosophy of the *Everson* opinion.

A problem of the no-aid aspect of the strict theory of separation advanced in *Everson* is to determine when a state is giving aid to religion and when it is levying a tax in support of religious activities. Does this mean the kind of aid that is distinctively and directly aimed at promotion of religion as such? Or does it embrace a wider idea, namely, that no aid can be given to religious institutions or activities even though it is incidental to a general governmental program designed to serve an appropriate secular interest? The assistance given to parochial schools by transporting students at public expense could be construed as an aid to religion. The four dissenting justices in *Everson* thought it was a form of forbidden aid.[32] Nevertheless, the court concluded that this was only indirect aid to religion, since the purpose was to provide safe transportation of children to schools which children were attending in compliance with compulsory education laws. In other words, the purpose was seen to be secular and incidental to the requirements of a law properly directed to secular objectives.

The first problem, then, in the application of the no-aid idea is to see whether or not government is directing its purposes to an appropriate secular end. This was made clear in the Sunday closing cases where, as the Court saw it, the purpose was to promote the appropriate secular objective of having a single day of rest during the week.[33] The fact that the Christian religion was benefited because Sunday is also the day of worship for Christians was seen to be incidental to the general purpose of the statute. On the other hand, it is clear that a literal application of the *Everson* doctrine requires the invalidation of a governmental program which is directed to the end of aiding or promoting a religious activity as such. Indeed, this is the only situation in which the *Everson* theory has been relied upon explicitly or implicitly to invalidate state action. In *McCollum* the clear purpose of the released time program was to facilitate participation by public school children in religious instruction conducted by church authorities. The same is true of *Engel* where the government was deliberately furthering a religious exercise in the interests of religious objectives. None of these cases is precedent then for an application of the no-aid idea to invalidate legislation which involves the use of public monies in support of secular educational objectives, even though there is an element of aid to religion in the picture.

Still, the question may be raised—in the light of *Everson*—whether any kind of direct relationship between government and churches is barred if it results in financial assistance, even though the relationship arises from a nonpreferential program aimed at a secular purpose. Two arguments are still available to limit the incidental or indirect aid doctrine relied on in *Everson* and the Sunday closing cases. One is that government may not lend aid or support to religious institutions or activities pursuant to a general secular program if government itself thereby becomes deeply involved in religious affairs. This defeats the purpose of the separation principle. This argument is most commonly advanced by those who rely upon the general proposition stated in *Everson* in contending that governmental support of parochial schools is unconstitutional. A second argument is that government in advancing a secular purpose may not employ religious means or instrumentalities to achieve its purpose if other alternatives are available. This could mean, for instance, that government, in providing support for health and education, may not extend this support to church-related hospitals and schools if public and nonreligious private institutions are adequate to serve these needs. These possible arguments help to point up the ambiguity of the *Everson* opinion, when tested by the result actually reached in that case. But again it should be emphasized that to date the no-aid principle has been applied to invalidate governmental action only where such action was expressly directed to religious ends.

2. *The Neutrality Theory.* The concept of neutrality as a key to the First Amendment's religion clauses received central attention in the court's recent opinions in the cases involving the recitation of the Lord's Prayer and the reading of the Bible without comment in public schools.[34] Although the court had before it the precedent of the *Engel* case, Mr. Justice Clark, who wrote the majority opinion, chose to rest the case on a theory not advanced in *Engel.* After reviewing all the cases, he said that what the Constitution requires is neutrality, which he described as a "wholesome neutrality." As stated by Mr. Justice Clark in the *Schemp* case, the test is as follows: "What are the purpose and the primary effect of the enactment? If either is the advancement or inhibition of religion then the enactment exceeds the scope of legislative power as circumscribed by the Constitution. That is to say that to withstand the strictures of the Establishment Clause there must be a secular legislative purpose and a primary effect that neither advances nor inhibits religion." [35] Neutrality so conceived means that laws and governmental programs must be directed to secular ends and must have a primary effect that neither advances nor inhibits religion. Although the language of primary effect is somewhat ambiguous, it suggests that in advancing secular ends government must not employ means that are essentially religious in character. Thus, the public schools in advancing a program directed to good citizenship may not employ a prayer exercise to achieve this end. It is the use of a distinctively religious means that creates the primary effect of advancing religion.

The test as stated by Mr. Justice Clark can then be viewed as embodying a theory of strict neutrality, namely, that the government may not use the religious factor as a basis for classification with the purpose of advancing or inhibiting religion. So interpreted, the theory propounded by Mr. Justice Clark appears to adopt the test proposed by Professor Philip Kurland, who has advanced a distinctive thesis for interpreting the First Amendment's twin religious phrases.[36] Professor Kurland's thesis, referred to already in the second chapter, is that the free exercise and the establishment clauses taken together state a coherent principle of classification, namely, that religion may not be used as a basis for classification in order to aid or hinder religious activity. The effect of these two clauses is to neutralize the religious factor as a basis of governmental classification. The free exercise clause, then, does not state an independent substantive concept of religious liberty but makes clear that there shall be no discrimination on religious grounds in the enjoyment of legal rights and privileges. In turn, the establishment clause precludes aid to religion as such but not aid extended to religious activities incidental to a broader classification which rests on a legitimate secular basis.

References to neutrality had appeared in the Supreme Court's opinions before Mr. Justice Clark advanced it as the central thesis for interpreting the establishment clause. In *Zorach* Mr. Justice Douglas said that the state must be neutral as between religious groups.[37] This is an entirely different concept of neutrality. Then later in his concurring opinion in *Schempp,* Mr. Justice Douglas speaks of neutrality as between believers and nonbelievers.[38] This is a much broader idea of neutrality. Others have deemed the neutrality concept essential to the interpretation of the First Amendment. Professor Wilber Katz of the University of Wisconsin law school, who

stresses religious liberty as the central value served by the
religion clauses of the First Amendment and who views the
separation principle as an instrument for advancing religious
liberty, reaches the position that government must be neutral.[39]
Governmental neutrality does serve the end of religious liberty
because it prevents the government from favoring religion over
nonreligion or one religious group over another. But Professor
Katz assumes that the free exercise and establishment limitations are separate and independent and may at times converge
on the same result and may at other times compete with each
other. It is in the latter case that Professor Katz interprets
the neutrality idea to mean that in some instances in order to
be utterly neutral the government must give aid to religion in
order to avoid placing religion at a disadvantage and thereby
limiting the full enjoyment of religious liberty. It is evident then
that "neutrality" may mean a number of different things.

In what respect does the neutrality principle advanced in
Schempp differ from the no-aid principle set forth in *Everson?*
Insofar as under both tests government can do nothing to aid
religion as such, that is, give religious activity a special preferential treatment, they point to the same result. But if the no-
aid test of *Everson* means that government can do nothing
which in fact aids religion, even though the governmental program is not directed to distinctively religious ends, it cuts a
wider swath than the neutrality test, which does not forbid aid
to religion so long as neither the purpose nor the means chosen
are distinctively identified in religious terms. But if the no-aid
test is limited by the principle that government in advancing
a secular purpose may incidentally aid religion, there is then
no apparent difference in the results reached under the two
different tests so far as aid to religion is concerned. The
critical difference between the two is that the no-aid test—
derived from the establishment clause—is directed only to

inquiring whether government is acting in aid of religion, whereas the neutrality test is further concerned with the question of whether government by its laws and programs is subjecting religion to a special disadvantage.

3. *The Accommodation Theory.* What I have chosen to call the accommodation theory found its first expression in *Zorach* v. *Clauson,* where the Supreme Court held that a state could authorize an arrangement whereby public school children could be released one hour a week for religious instruction off the school premises.[40] The court here distinguished *McCollum,* which had held a released time arrangement invalid if conducted in public school classrooms. It was evident that the court was making a distinction based on the relative degree of involvement by the public school system in the program, finding that the involvement here was not too great when public school property itself was not used for this purpose. Three judges who had participated in the majority result in the *McCollum* case dissented on the ground that the majority reasoning in *Zorach* had missed what they thought was the main point in *McCollum,* namely, that the school system was being used in order to facilitate religious instruction.[41] This was undoubtedly the case, and many commentators thought at the time that the effect of the *Zorach* opinion was to weaken considerably the rigidity and absoluteness that had characterized the broad statement in *Everson* and its application in *McCollum.*[42]

Of even greater interest was the general tone of Mr. Justice Douglas' opinion in *Zorach,* which suggested a more moderate approach to the interpretation of the establishment clause than indicated by the broad sweeping ideas found in the *Everson* opinion. Indeed, the flavor of the *Zorach* case cannot be fully appreciated without quoting part of Mr. Justice Douglas' opinion:

There is much talk of the separation of church and state in the history of the Bill of Rights and in the decisions clustering around the First Amendment. . . . There cannot be the slightest doubt that the First Amendment reflects a philosophy that church and state should be separated. And so far as interference with the "free exercise" of religion and the "establishment" of religion are concerned, the separation must be complete and unequivocal. The First Amendment within the scope of its coverage permits no exception; the prohibition is absolute. The First Amendment, however, does not say that in every and all respects there shall be a separation of church and state. Rather, it studiously defines the manner, the specific ways, in which there shall be no concert or union, or dependency one on the other. That is the common sense of the matter. Otherwise state and religions would be aliens to each other—hostile, suspicious, and even unfriendly. Churches could not even be required to pay property taxes. Municipalities would not be permitted to render police or fire protection to religious groups. Policemen who help parishioners into their places of worship would violate the Constitution. Prayers in our legislative halls; the appeal to the Almighty in the message of the chief executives; the proclamation making Thanksgiving Day a holiday; "So help me God" in our courtroom oaths—these and all other references to the Almighty that run through our laws, our public rituals, our ceremonies would be flouting the First Amendment. A fastidious atheist or agnostic could even object to the supplication with which the court opens each session: "God save the United States and this honorable Court."

. . . We are a religious people whose institutions presuppose a Supreme Being. We guarantee the freedoms to worship as one chooses. We make room for as wide a variety of beliefs and creeds as the spiritual needs of man deem necessary. We sponsor an attitude on the part of government that shows no partiality to any one group and that lets each flourish according to zeal of its adherents and the appeal of its dogma. When the state encourages religious instruction or cooperates with religious authorities by adjusting the schedule of public events to sectarian needs, it follows the best of our traditions. For it then respects the religious nature of our people and accommodates the public service to their spiritual needs. To hold that it may not would be to find in the Constitution a requirement that the government show a callous indifference to religious groups. That would be preferring those who believe in no religion over those who do believe. Government may not finance religious groups nor undertake religious instruction or blend secular and sectarian education nor use secular institutions to force one or some religion on any person. But we find no constitutional requirement which makes it necessary for government to be hostile to religion and to throw its weight against efforts to widen the effective scope of religious influence. The government must be neutral when it comes to competition between sects. It may not thrust any sect on any person. It may not make a religious observance compulsory. It may not coerce any person to attend church, to observe a religious holiday, or to take religious instruction. But it can close its doors or suspend its operations as to those who want to repair to their religious sanctuary for worship or instruction. No more than that is undertaken here.

. . . The constitutional standard is a separation of church and state. The problem, like many problems in Constitutional Law, is one of degree.[43]

This interesting language from *Zorach* is quoted at length because it reveals an attitude which recognizes that there are necessary interrelationships between government and religion, that the government cannot be indifferent to religion in American life, and that far from being hostile or even neutral, it may accommodate its institutions and its programs to the religious interests of the people. Moreover, the court in *Zorach* undertook to approach the problems under the establishment clause in the same pragmatic way in which it deals with other constitutional questions, that is, by weighing and appraising various competing interests and striking a balance through the judicial process. This is revealed in the statement that the First Amendment requires a separation of church and state only to the extent that this grows from interpretation and application of the free exercise and the establishment clauses and the recognition that the questions here presented are questions of degree. The court found that the states' legitimate concern with the freedom of parents to give their children religious education outweighed any involvement by the state in religious instruction through the use of the public school system. The court drew the line, then, between a system which permits religious instruction in the public schools and that which facilitates such instruction outside of school property but at the expense of school time. The court recognized that such a program could not be forced on children and that coercion could not be used to compel children to participate, but implicit in its decision was a rejection of the idea that coercion to attend released time classes inhered in the system.

It is clear that the accommodation theory points to results different from those reached under the no-aid and neutrality tests. Under these latter tests the system of released time at issue was clearly invalid. Here the government was party to a program designed to advance religious ends. The accommodation approach of *Zorach* reflects a pragmatism in striking contrast to the conceptualism that underlies the no-aid and strict neutrality principles.

The accommodation theory offers some distinctive advantages as a vehicle for interpreting the religion clauses of the First Amendment. In the first place, it takes account of various long-accepted historical practices, for example, the military chaplaincy, tax exemptions for houses of worship and for property used for religious purposes, prayers in legislative halls, and recognition of the religious nature and interests of our people as expressed in inscriptions on our coins, Presidential Thanksgiving proclamations, and prayers on public occasions. These historical practices help to illuminate the meaning of separation of church and state as a constitutional principle.

Secondly, the accommodation concept is a useful vehicle for relating the establishment limitation to the free exercise clause. It proceeds on the assumption that these are two independent substantive limitations and that the no-establishment principle cannot be used to jeopardize the free exercise of religion. I refer again to the interpretation of the free exercise clause which supports the conclusion that in some instances government may, and in others must, grant a preferred treatment to religious liberty.[44] Obviously any preferred treatment of religious liberty that authorizes or requires special privileges on religious grounds under regulatory and tax laws of general application cannot be squared with a strict no-aid theory. Likewise, any preferred treatment of religious liberty cannot be reconciled with the strict neutrality theory, which precludes any use of the religious factor as a basis for classification in order either to aid or hinder religion. An accommodation theory, on the other hand, recognizes that any principle of no-aid or neutrality derived from the establishment limitation must yield in order to assure the full enjoyment of religious liberty or to permit the legislature a discretionary authority to implement this liberty. In short, the accommodation theory recognizes the larger neutrality proposed by Professor Katz.

I have singled out three theories distilled from the Supreme Court's opinions interpreting the establishment clause—the no-aid theory, the strict neutrality theory, and the accommodation theory. The critical question is which theory the court is presently following or is likely to follow in the future. One must be careful in speculating about the mind of the court, particularly in an area where a variety of views have been expressed. At no time has the court disowned or repudiated ideas expressed in earlier cases. Certainly it would be inaccurate to say that the broad ideas of no-aid stated in *Everson* have been repudiated. Indeed, the court in its latest opinion in

Schempp quoted at length from all the prior opinions beginning with *Everson*. But in the *Schempp* opinion the court used a formal test of strict neutrality. *Zorach* was decided before *Schempp,* so it may be concluded that at present the court is committed to the strict neutrality doctrine and has disowned the theory of accommodation. It would be erroneous, however, to jump to this conclusion.

In the first place, the treatment of neutrality in Mr. Justice Clark's opinion in *Schempp* is more ambiguous than appears from the formal test he propounded. He spoke with apparent approval of public practices that recognize the place of religion in our national life. In condemning the prayer and Bible-reading exercises in public schools, he did not find it enough to say that here the government was sanctioning a practice directed to religious ends, but went on to emphasize the elements of compulsion in this case. He noted that the prayer was approved by state authorities, was prescribed for daily use in a public school for children required to attend under the compulsory education laws, and was supervised by a state employee—the public school teacher. If strict neutrality were the criterion, then it should have been unnecessary for the court to discuss the elements of compulsion in that case. But if compulsion is the key factor, then is the court not saying that the state cannot be a party to practices that have the effect of compelling the acceptance of religious ideas or of exposing people to a compulsory religious practice at the possible expense of impairing their own freedom of conscience? If the rationale of establishment is that government cannot use its powers to compel acceptance of belief, then consideration of the freedoms protected under the free exercise and establishment clauses is central to their interpretation. Government can be less than neutral in many ways respecting religious matters without coercing conscience or violating individual freedom.

Moreover, the court in *Schempp* went out of its way to distinguish the *Zorach* case where the court had upheld released time off school premises. It found that not all the same elements of compulsion common to the prayer and Bible-reading cases were present in the released time situation. Since it can be argued that government is not being strictly neutral when it uses the public school system as a means of furthering religious instruction even though it be off the school premises, it seems fair to say that the total opinion in *Schempp* is more consistent with the benevolent neutrality inspired by the accommodation principle than with the test of strict neutrality formally stated in the opinion. Even more revealing, however, are the separate opinions in the *Schempp* case.

Mr. Justice Brennan wrote a long concurring opinion in which he, more than any other single justice in the court to date, recognized the possibility of conflict between the establishment and free exercise clauses and developed the accommodation doctrine as a means of reconciling the two clauses.[45] Indeed, he accepts the idea that some accommodations between church and state and between government and religion are necessary, and he recognizes that these accommodations have played a part in our national life. He lists a series of permissible accommodation categories as well as categories where accommodation is required for religious liberty. Mr. Justice Brennan has therefore squarely planted his feet in the accommodation camp. Mr. Justice Goldberg in a separate opinion, joined by Mr. Justice Harlan, made clear that insofar as neutrality means that government can do nothing to accommodate itself to the religious factor in American life, it does not state a tenable doctrine.[46] Mr. Justice Stewart, who had dissented in *Engel*,[47] dissented at greater length in *Schempp*.[48] Rejecting what he called a doctrinaire and mechanistic application of the separation concept, he was willing to accept prayer and Bible-reading exercises in public schools as a permissible accommodation by government to the religious interests of the people, provided that no religion received preferential treatment and that children were free from compulsion to take part in these programs.

So at least four justices of the court in *Schempp* explicitly recognized that unbending neutrality should not be applied and that the constitutional principle of separation of church and state admitted of the flexibility of the accommodation theory.

Further illumination is provided by the opinions in the *Sherbert* case.[49] There the court held that the state of South Carolina was required, in the interest of religious liberty, to accommodate its unemployment compensation laws to the religious beliefs of Seventh-Day Adventists. Here was a case of required accommodation of the state's policy to religious liberty even though it invited charges that by strict application of establishment ideas, the state was establishing Seventh-Day Adventism as the religion of the state. This argument is relevant according to strict no-aid or strict neutrality principles. To be sure, some members of the court joined in the opinion even though they have in the past expressed themselves in favor of the strict no-aid idea. This again makes clear that even the no-aid principle must always be construed with reference to the competing values of the free exercise clause. While agreeing wholeheartedly with the result, Mr. Justice Stewart in his concurring opinion in *Sherbert* said that this accommodation to religious freedom was hardly compatible with the rigid application of the establishment clause, which the majority had supported in the *Engel* and the *Schempp* cases.[50] Mr. Justice Harlan, dissenting in *Sherbert,* stated that although he agreed that there could be no strict application of the neutrality idea because of the numerous interrelationships of law and religion in American life and although some accommodations

were essential, it was, nevertheless, going too far to say that
the Constitution actually required this kind of accommodation
by South Carolina to the religious views of Seventh-Day
Adventists.[51] Mr. Justice White concurred in Justice Harlan's
dissenting opinion. It appears then that a majority of the court
recognize the validity of the accommodation principle in the
interpretation of the First Amendment's religion clauses.

It would be a mistake, however, to suggest that the theory
of accommodation which seems to be accepted by the majority
of the court is unrelated to other ideas and theories that have
been developed, notably the no-aid and neutrality concepts.
Rather, accommodation, instead of being viewed as a wholly
independent theory of interpretation, should be seen as a modi-
fication of the no-aid or neutrality concepts. The justices who
follow the strict no-aid idea are indeed forced to recognize
that the free exercise principle does sometimes enter in as a
competing force, but in these situations they may rest their
case entirely on free exercise without recognizing a subordina-
tion of the establishment limitation. Likewise, it seems clear—
and this is made evident in the opinions in *Schempp*—that
justices who recognize the validity of the accommodation idea
expressed in *Zorach* may still assume that, in general, government must be neutral in religious matters or that government may not generally lend its aid to distinctively religious
forces.

These ideas cannot be pressed to their absolute limit. Not
only must the no-aid or neutrality concept be subordinated to
the necessities of free exercise, but an area of legislative discretion must be allowed where a state may choose to advance
the cause of religious freedom even at the expense of not being
completely neutral. Indeed, this may be described as the larger
or benevolent neutrality. It should be recognized also that in
some situations the court can agree on the result in a case

whether it uses a strict no-aid theory or a strict neutrality theory or whether it follows either of these theories tempered by accommodation. In the *Schempp* case the members of the court who subscribed to the more flexible pragmatic position of accommodation thought it would be pushing accommodation too far to permit the state to require religious exercises in public schools. Likewise, it would be running the accommodation theory into the ground and unduly subordinating the establishment limitation to the free exercise guarantee to suggest that a state may accommodate itself to the religious needs of the people by granting money in direct support of churches or by granting money exclusively directed to the support of religious institutions. The choice, then, is not strictly between no-aid or neutrality, on the one hand, and accommodation, on the other. Rather, an approach to the First Amendment is needed which recognizes that the separation principle cannot be given an absolute application, that account can be taken of historical practices, that the necessity is always present of balancing and weighing the respective interests which are to be protected under the twin clauses of the First Amendment.

Such a pragmatic rather than conceptual approach offers a more viable judicial technique for dealing with the complex interests of current situations. The wall of separation metaphor, useful as it is to symbolize the respective functions of church and state, serves only to disguise and obscure the complexity of the issues if it is converted into an absolute principle that fails to take account either of the interrelationship of free exercise and establishment or of the interrelationship of government and churches in areas of common concern.

If the accommodation concept is used to temper the rigidities of both the no-aid and strict neutrality theories, then the ultimate problem the court faces is to determine the respective values served by the twin religion clauses of the First Amendment and to resolve the dilemma that arises when the values served by the twin clauses are seen to conflict. A useful starting point is to recognize that religious liberty—broadly conceived to include all varieties of religious belief and freedom of total belief and nonbelief—is the central value served by both clauses. Whatever else government may or may not do, it is required to respect religious liberty. This means, first of all, that it must refrain from laws that restrict the free exercise of religion or which discriminate on religious grounds in the granting of rights or privileges, unless clearly defined policy grounds warrant such discrimination. It further means that since religious liberty occupies a preferred position in the constellation of constitutional freedoms, the legislature in exercising its discretionary authority may in some situations grant a special advantage or immunity on religious grounds in order to facilitate the free exercise of religion.

But what considerations derived from the establishment clause, in terms of no-aid or neutrality, limit the freedom to further religious liberty? To state this limitation is to recognize that the Constitution may either require, permit, or prohibit the state from accommodating its laws and programs to the furtherance of religious liberty. But how does the court determine whether given governmental action fits into a particular category? It is at this point that the idea of undue "involvement" by the state in religious matters plays a significant role. The concurring opinions by Justices Brennan and Goldberg in *Schempp* are particularly illuminating. It is also useful to recall what Mr. Justice Brennan said in *Sherbert* where the court held that a state was required to grant an exemption on religious grounds in its unemployment compensation law. In rejecting the argument that the court was thereby compelling the state to establish a particular religion, it said that this concession to religious liberty did not represent "that involvement of religious with secular institutions which it was the object of the Establishment Clause to forestall" and did not abridge any other person's religious liberties. Devotion to the larger neutrality stops at the point where government by its own laws and programs becomes unduly involved in religious matters. Government is too deeply involved when it grants general subsidies to churches, since it is thereby sanctioning religious beliefs and forcing nonbelievers to pay taxes in support of doctrines they do not accept. Government is too deeply involved when it prescribes religious practices in public schools, since a variety of compulsive factors are present that threaten the liberty of the nonconformist. Government is too deeply involved when it authorizes released time on the school premises, for again a number of compulsive factors are present. The degree of governmental participation in the sanctioning or support of religious practices and the corresponding impact upon freedom of belief and conscience are then the critical factors which enter into the determination of undue involvement. This involvement must, in turn, be weighed against the demands of religious liberty. Support of the military chaplaincy, for example, means some governmental involvement in religious matters and may offend the conscience of some taxpayers; but here government is not prescribing any particular belief or coercing the conscience of soldiers, but is acting to promote religious liberty in a special situation.

Where the issue is not the use of governmental power to sanction religious belief and practices by some positive program but the granting of exemption on religious grounds from laws of general operation, what determines whether the government is required, or permitted, to make the accommodation? While a state may appropriately grant exemptions from its general police and tax laws, it should not be constitutionally required to do so unless this immunity can properly be claimed as part of the constitutional guarantee of religious liberty. Thus, exemptions from property tax and military service, health and labor laws should be at the discretion of government. Whether *Sherbert* carried the principle of required accommodation too far is debatable. It may well be that the court here undertook a determination of questions better left to the legislature and that in this area, as in the case of the Sunday closing laws, the policy of granting exemptions on religious grounds should be left to legislative discretion.

Whether the issue is called no-aid, neutrality, or accommodation without undue involvement, the terms used and the concepts employed by the Supreme Court are tools for giving meaning to the establishment clause. Any interpretation of this clause and the constitutional values it serves must also take account of the free exercise clause and the values it serves. This accounts in substantial part for the complexity of the problems presented before the courts during constitutional litigation. Underlying the issues as related in legal terms and the theories used in resolving them are basic values and policies which guide the courts. Neither constitutional language, nor history, nor precedent furnishes answers to these questions. These policies reveal the nature of American society. What the court says and holds reflects not only the competing interests and values at stake, but also its own role in accommodating constitutional interpretation to the demands of a pluralistic society.

4

GOVERNMENT AND RELIGION:

Accommodation
in a Pluralistic Society

In the first chapter I pointed to features of our national religious, social, and political development which require the churches to re-examine their position with respect to each other and to the social and political order. I noted the emergence of the new pluralism and the problem it raises of the contribution of the churches to the national consensus, and I called attention to the expanded activities of government in welfare and education—areas in which the churches have traditionally manifested great interest.

In the second chapter I dealt with the concept of religious liberty as central to the place of religion in the constitutional order, and in the third chapter I discussed the interpretation of the establishment clause and its significance for governmental recognition and support of religion, with particular respect to the protection and promotion of religious liberty. The new social, religious, and political developments cannot be divorced from the constitutional development as expressed in the Supreme Court's decisions. They call for reappraisal of practices and usages sanctioned by history. I suggest, for instance, that the recent decisions dealing with the time-honored practices of prayer and Bible-reading in public schools reflect the Supreme Court's appreciation of contemporary pluralism and the decline of Protestant hegemony. Likewise, the use of the Fourteenth Amendment to make the establishment clause apply to the states reflects basically the expanding nationalism and declining localism of our common life. In turn, the constitutional interpretations furnish an important part of the total setting within which the churches may assess their position vis-à-vis the civil community and the government in areas of common concern. In short, the question for consideration in this chapter is: How do the churches and the government accommodate themselves to the new order in the totality of its social, religious, political, and constitutional features?

I turn first to the contribution the churches make to the nation's common life or, as sometimes put, the consensus or underlying moral objectives or common faith of the country. This discussion is premised on the assumption that religion is not simply a private matter that concerns only an individual's relationship to a Creator, but that it transcends one's personal belief and expresses itself in ethical attitudes and social conduct. It is premised on the assumption also that the churches in their corporate capacity have an impact on the mind of the community and on the principles which should be reflected in laws and legislative programs. In short, this discussion proceeds on the assumption that religion is relevant to life and therefore to our secular, political, and constitutional order.

The first consideration of importance to the churches is the maintenance of the conditions of religious liberty. It is not necessary to stress this point at length, since it is an affirmation of ideas expressed in the second chapter. But it is important for the churches to remember that a wholehearted devotion to the principle of religious liberty is indispensable to their freedom. This means that the churches must be free to carry on their function, to interpret and to proclaim truth in accordance with their understanding, to engage in the corporate life of the church that sustains the faith, to teach and instruct their members in the elements of the faith, and to bear witness to the relevancy of the faith in matters of social concern. This centrality of religious liberty serves as the starting point in determining the relation of the churches to the government. It means both the freedom to proclaim their truth and to carry on their activities free from governmental restraint, and the freedom from involvements with the state which prejudice and compromise the churches in the exercise of their prophetic function or which impair the voluntaristic character of their enterprises and in effect convert them into secular enterprises.

The churches also face the necessity—all the more acute and imperative in a pluralistic society—of emphasizing the voluntaristic character of religious faith. They must recognize that they cannot depend upon government to achieve their purposes or to bolster their faith. A religion relevant to the life of the individual and of the community must be founded upon the spirit. Religion is not true to itself if it depends upon governmental prescription and coercion. The churches cannot look to the government to perform their tasks. Some of the current discussions fail to recognize that the churches are free only when they can depend upon their own spiritual resources both in ministering to the lives of their communicants and in bearing witness to this in the life of the community.

As suggested in the second chapter, the free and voluntaristic nature of religion as a spiritual force involves full freedom of belief and disbelief. This freedom is impaired when government uses its coercive power to sanction religious faith. The churches must not only assert the freedom of the churches to proclaim their message and bear witness and the freedom of the individual to express his religious faith, but the freedom to disavow faith as well. Because religious liberty is at times so closely identifiable with the related freedoms of speech, press, and assembly, the churches have an interest in supporting and championing freedom in all of its aspects. For the same reason the churches must understand that it is in their best interest to remain free from government involvements that tempt the church to weaken its message or which encourage the use of governmental powers to advance religious interests.

Consistent with this emphasis on religious liberty and the recognition that the best interests of church and state are served when each is true to its own functions, the churches are in a position to appraise their contribution to the common life and to the common faith. It is not the business of the churches— and here let me speak particularly of the Christian churches— to seek to make a Christian state out of the nation or to Christianize the law. State, government, and law are necessarily secular in character. The positive law and the institutions of government are concerned not with correct belief but with overt conduct related to good order, peace, justice, freedom, and community welfare. Churches transgress their proper function when they attempt to impose their own peculiar moral beliefs derived from religious insight upon others who do not share these beliefs and insights. It is imperative that in our pluralistic society no church seek the sanction of law for its own moral conceptions unless they are translatable into moral values and social policy appropriate to the purposes of the secular community. Churches are tempted to seek legislative sanction for their moral insights and thereby to impose their will upon the whole community. This leads them to ignore the fact that secular government is concerned with moral motivation only insofar as it relates to overt conduct prejudicial to the interests and values served by the law. They tend to disregard the freedom of those whose moral attitudes are totally different. I have in mind not only the attempts of the Catholic church to influence legislation in such matters as birth control, sterilization, marriage, and divorce, but also the tendency of Protestant churches when in a dominant position to seek legislation on such matters as Sunday closing, gambling, and prohibition.[1]

Yet it should also be clear that the cultivation of moral insights and values is indeed a function of religious faith and the churches, and it is the business of the churches to speak with a prophetic voice in addressing themselves to the conditions of our day. They have a contribution to make to the moral consensus of the community. The law reflects moral ends and moral choices. Citizens whose awareness of moral values is conditioned by religious insight necessarily help shape this moral choice. They can cheerfully join with others in upholding and championing the human and social values served by our democratic society and thereby translate religious faith into community actions consistent with the ends of the secular society. Religion is relevant to the law and to the community consensus.

The separation principle does not mean that religion is irrelevant to political life and to law. The notion that churches must stay out of politics is valid only insofar as it expresses the idea that the church must not identify itself with the state, use its influence as a political force to control the action of government, or use the force of numbers to impose its moral views on the community. It is an invalid idea if it suggests that the churches and individual church members cannot draw upon their moral resources and insights to contribute to the goals of the secular community. In the solution to the great problems we face today, the Judeo-Christian understanding of the worth and dignity of man—his freedom as a moral creature and the conditions essential to the fulfillment of human needs—has much to say in defining the ethos of our democratic order.

It is in these considerations that we may find some answers to the question of how the churches accommodate themselves to the contemporary religious pluralism. No one church can impose its will on the community. Each church to be true to itself must maintain the cutting edge of its own witness. Yet there is room for dialogue in the search for understanding, not only with respect to matters of faith, but also with respect to the basic moral presuppositions underlying the values served by our democratic society. The churches have a contribution to make through their spiritual ministry and witness to the consensus that informs our democratic order and can cooperate with each other and with secular groups in advancing the values established by this consensus. And perhaps, most important of all, they have a basis for cultivating a common respect and loyalty to the constitutional order that insures religious freedom and the opportunity for religion to make its impact upon the common life. They all have an interest in the civic peace that prevails when each church recognizes the freedom of other churches to express their insight into religious truth.

Certainly the quest for consensus should not be directed to the promotion of a new common denominator religion that dilutes and weakens the historic faiths. Reference was made in the introductory remarks to the popularity of religion today and the cultivation of an American folk religion that identifies faith in God with the American culture and the American way of life. This is a dangerous confusion of religion with the existing order, with the result that religion is secularized and its cutting edge lost. It is neither in the quest for a common religion nor in the promotion of a vague religiosity identified with patriotism that the churches find a meaningful basis of consensus. Rather, they should create the moral leaven that infuses the secular order and should support the civic values and goals compatible with the insights of faith.

At this point it is appropriate to bring up the question of secularism in our national life. Is is easy to mention the secular with disapproval or even contempt as though in itself it were an antireligious force or something evil. Christians recognize that secular authority and the secular order are part of God's creation and under his sovereignty and law. Secularism in the authentic sense means that the ordering of the social life is in the hands of a community and of a government that is directed toward secular ends. The state as the instrument of secular authority is not concerned with man's spiritual redemption. There is nothing unholy or evil about the secular in this sense. Because government, laws, and constitutional systems are essential to the secular order and have their own valid function to perform, the churches can and should cheerfully respect and support the government's secular objectives. Our problem is that we constantly fail to differentiate between secularism as a term that describes the essentially secular character of our culture and its institutions, such as government and law, and secularism as a philosophy that rests on the notion that any belief in God is irrelevant to life and that man can by his own efforts achieve his own salvation or at least that he must be content to operate wholly within the framework of his own aspirations and resources.

Sometimes the term secularistic is used to describe a program that makes a philosophy or religion out of secularism. Government must be secular, but it is not the government's business to promote a secularistic philosophy. Although it is clear that government must necessarily be secular, it does not follow that the secular government must be indifferent to the religious faiths and traditions of its people. It is the function and responsibility of the secular state to maintain a hospitable climate for religious liberty, whether we view religious liberty as a necessary means of expression of the spiritual life or whether we see it wholly as a civic liberty essential to the maintenance of peace. Beyond this it is appropriate for government through its secular institutions to take account of the relevancy of religion in the national life. We may here use as a text for further discussion the oft quoted passage from Mr. Justice Douglas' opinion in the *Zorach* case: "We are a religious people whose institutions presuppose a Supreme Being." [2]

This passage has been quoted so often that its truthfulness is assumed without question. Actually this statement says two things. First of all, it says that we are a religious people. This is a statement of fact which is either true or not true. Whether we are a religious people, as distinguished from a religious state or a religious government, is a matter capable of some determination, if we can agree that formal expression of religious belief, membership in religious organizations, and religious activity as generally understood is an indication of the religious character of the people. Judged by these criteria we are a religious people. But the second part of Mr. Justice Douglas' statement raises more questions. Professor Sidney Hook has said that this statement is manifestly untrue since there is nothing to indicate that our institutions—particularly our constitutional and governmental institutions—necessarily rest on the assumption that there is a Supreme Being. [3] It is true, as he says, that a state directed to secular ends can rest on assumptions that are not necessarily identified with religious belief. But I think that in a very large sense Mr. Justice Douglas' statement was correct when he said that our institu-

tions presuppose a Supreme Being. For many people in this
country past and present, our institutions do have a religious
significance. That not all accept their religious significance is
immaterial.

Many Christians believe that government and laws are part
of God's created order. According to this notion our institutions do presuppose a Supreme Being. But even more con-
cretely, we can point to many facets of American life which
support the conclusion that at least for a large segment of our
population religious ideas are deemed essential to our institutions. The Declaration of Independence with its assertion that
all men are created equal and endowed by the Creator with
certain inalienable rights is a religious view of the source and
nature of man's rights. The frequent references to religion in
our great historic documents, the preambles to our state constitutions acknowledging dependence upon God, and the mani-
festations of religion in public life all support a judicial recognition that in the thinking of many people our institutions do
presuppose a Supreme Being. Our coins carry the inscription
"In God We Trust," and the pledge of allegiance speaks of
this nation "under God."

Much more significant is what government can do to recognize in its public practices and in its educational institutions
the relevancy of religion in the lives of its citizens. This is a
matter of genuine concern, for it raises the question of whether
government by indifference to religion is not being more than
neutral and is exercising its secular authority to promote irre-
ligion. It is not the government's business to prescribe or under-
write any kind of official faith or ideology. In his famous
opinion in the *Barnette* case Mr. Justice Jackson said that if
there is one star in our constellation it is that no official "can
prescribe what shall be orthodox in politics, nationalism, religion, or other matters of opinion or force citizens to confess

by word or act their faith therein." [4] This idea has very significant implications since it suggests that even apart from the specific language of the First Amendment concerning an establishment of religion, there is an implied limitation in the First Amendment against the establishment by government of any kind of belief or ideology. To say, however, that government cannot prescribe an official national faith or ideology brings us face to face with current problems of the public schools. Can government successfully maintain its position as a secular state and be neutral in religious matters and yet avoid the charge that by its failure to promote religion it is thereby establishing secularism as a national faith? The answer to this must necessarily be yes. No other answer is consistent with the conception of a secular state and with the presuppositions of a religiously pluralistic society. Yet the question also suggests that to be really neutral, government cannot ignore the relevancy of religion in American life. How to recognize this relevancy without making itself a party to the prescription of religious belief poses difficult and delicate problems.

It is in the context of the public school system that this problem assumes particular significance. The really critical issues that have come before the Supreme Court on the interpretation of the establishment clause have been concerned with education at the primary and secondary levels. The only cases in which the court has held governmental practices invalid under the establishment clause are those in which the court declared public school practices—released time for religious instruction[5] and prayer and Bible-reading exercises[6]—to be unconstitutional.[7]

These decisions indicate that religious practices in the public school and governmental support of parochial schools touch on the most sensitive area of church-state relations. As Mr. Justice Brennan stated in his concurrence in the *Schempp* case, the questions that the court dealt with in the recent prayer and Bible-reading cases are entirely peculiar to the public school and the place it occupies in American society.[8] This is not the occasion to develop at length the significance of public education. It can be justified entirely on the utilitarian ground that the state has an interest in a minimum education for all its citizens and that private agencies do not have the financial resources to meet this public need. But many consider the public school a pivotal institution not only for training children, but for promoting values central to our democratic society.[9] Because our schools are not to be segregated on the basis of race or religion, because persons of all classes come together in them, because they furnish the means for achieving civic unity despite the numerous diversities of our culture, the public schools occupy a unique place in our democratic society. The judicial position taken with respect to religious practices in public schools cannot be viewed in isolation from policy considerations rooted in an understanding of the functions and values served by the public school in a pluralistic society.

We must also consider the historical evolution of our public schools. They were developed at a time of Protestant domination, and some of the practices associated with them reflect a particular Protestant bias and concern. There is truth to the assertion that our public schools developed originally as Protestant schools.[10] The same Protestant groups that were unswerving in their opposition to the use of any public funds to support parochial schools found nothing incompatible with this position in supporting religious practices congenial to their own belief in the public schools. As long as the Protestant groups remained dominant, prayer and Bible-reading were deemed appropriate to the public schools. It is only in the contemporary era of religious pluralism, with the decline of Protestant influence, that these practices are challenged as no longer compatible with a system that recognizes freedom and equality of all religions and which places government in a position where it can support none.

This new awareness forces all churches to make a fresh appraisal of this problem and to realize, first of all, that instruction in religion, the inculcation of religious insight in dealing with life's problems, the development of spiritual and moral attitudes, and the promotion of religious devotion are the function of church and home. Yet there is also the well-supported feeling that the schools cannot be indifferent to the matter of religion, since religion has played a conspicuous role in shaping our institutions. Moreover, a studied indifference of religion does subject the public schools to the charge of a secularistic bias.

How the schools can deal with this is the crucial problem of our day. In its recent cases the Supreme Court has said that for the public schools to require religious practices, such as prayers and Bible-reading without comment, is a violation of the separation principle since government to this extent is establishing religion. Or to put the matter in the terms of the concurring judges in the *Schempp* case, the state is thereby too greatly involved in religious instruction to warrant this as a permissible accommodation of the state's program to religious liberty and religious interests.[11] Whether the Supreme Court acted wisely in deciding to review the prayer and Bible-reading cases and whether it reached a wise result will continue to be debatable matters. It requires a very broad interpretation of the establishment clause to say that these public school exercises amount to an establishment of religion. Nor can it be said without careful study that these exercises did not promote appropriate secular ends by serving as symbols of the nation's religious heritage and in contributing to good citizenship. Likewise, to deny that the reading of the Bible without comment has an educational as well as moral value is to engage in judgment without adequate documentation. These practices have had a long history in a number of states, and there is merit to the argument that practices of this kind should be left to local control, subject to state constitutional and statutory limitations, as long as they do not result in substantial impingement upon personal liberty. Whether, with the privilege of non-participation, there was such a substantial impingement upon personal liberty or such a significant encroachment upon freedom of conscience is a question on which reasonably minded persons may differ. Noncomformists suffer many disadvantages in our society, and as Mr. Justice Jackson pointed out in his concurring opinion in the *McCollum* case, our public school system would be reduced to fragments if public schools can be enjoined by courts from engaging in practices which are objectionable to minority groups.[12] Nor is it an answer to this argument that government may reflect the will of the majority in the public school system so long as the government is pursuing only appropriate secular objectives.

According to *Barnette*, government may not prescribe any kind of official belief, and force it upon students. Yet in the flag salute case a student objecting on religious grounds to an officially prescribed statement of belief was deemed to have his rights sufficiently protected by not being forced to participate. There was no suggestion that because of his objection the entire practice could be eliminated. Moreover, if we accept the broad interpretation of religion as suggested by some of the recent judicial opinions, almost any kind of ideological belief can be regarded as a form of religion, with the result that the prescription of even a political belief and the affirmation of democratic values can be viewed as an attempt to prescribe a religious practice.

Despite these considerations, however, the results reached

by the court in the prayer and Bible-reading cases can be supported on substantial grounds. The argument that these practices serve some secular values must be weighed against the consideration that the practices are essentially religious in character and that it is not the business of the government to make itself a party to official religious practices whether for the purpose of promoting secular or religious ends. Indeed, the deliberate use by government of religious means to promote secular objectives is a threat to the integrity and vitality of religion. What emerges in the end is some general common-denominator religion identified with civic virtues and the established secular order. Furthermore, such practices as prayer and Bible-reading in the public schools are essentially ritual-istic in nature, tend to become mechanical, and may, indeed, have the effect of debasing religion in the mind of the student. The tendency in the case of Bible-reading without comment to choose books or passages with the minimum of religious content in order to avoid offense to particular groups can result in a distorted picture of the Bible. The religionist and non-religionist alike have ground for objecting to a practice which gives an official status to a particular form of religious belief and expression and which puts the student at some disadvantage if he identifies himself as a nonconformist by electing not to take part in these practices. It is fair to say, in the interest of protecting individual liberty, that the public schools should not engage in practices involving affirmation of belief unless these practices are clearly identifiable as appropriate means for achieving legitimate secular purposes.

Finally, depending on the religious composition of the community, these practices do offend minority groups, arouse religious feelings, and promote community divisiveness. In short, they have a tendency to create many of the problems that arise when government is asked to use its compulsive force to support religion. At least it is not difficult to sense the policy considerations which led the court to resort to a broad construction of the establishment limitation as a vehicle for invalidating these practices. It should not be forgotten that Bible-reading had been declared invalid by some courts as a form of sectarian instruction forbidden by state constitutional provisions long before the problem came to be a federal constitutional issue.

Much of the criticism of recent cases turned on apprehensions that exaggerated or distorted the decisions. The court did not hold that all references to Deity in public life and all religious aspects of public ceremonies were unconstitutional. The decisions do not affect these matters or such practices as prayers at the beginning of legislative sessions. The elements of official involvement and compulsion that led the court to declare religious practices in the public schools unconstitutional are absent in these other situations. Finally, the decisions even in their application to the public school apply only to corporate religious practices prescribed by public authority. They did not invalidate patriotic exercises that include references to Deity or acknowledgment of dependence upon him. Nor do the decisions outlaw prayer in the classroom. Needless to say, an individual child is still free to pray! A school board may properly prescribe a period of silence and meditation in which a child may pray or read devotional literature. Indeed, it is possible that school boards may permit voluntary religious practices in public schools. Perhaps school boards can find ways of giving opportunity for wholly voluntary participation by students in religious exercises congenial to their own faith, having no stamp of official approval and not conducted by a teacher, so as to eliminate the principal elements of governmental involvement that were stressed in *Engel* and *Schempp*. This is the difference between prescribing religious practices and allowing opportunity for them and could be the difference between an unlawful governmental establishment of religion and a permissible accommodation in the interest of religious liberty.

Whether the Supreme Court would approve any such plan remains to be seen. Certainly it would put to the test the question of whether *Engel* and *Schempp* rested on the elements of compulsion stressed in those cases or whether they rested on a fundamental conception of the public schools and the necessity of maintaining them free from any kind of religious influence. A federal district court in a recent decision has held that parents, relying on the free exercise clause, have a constitutional right to have their children participate in a strictly voluntary prayer exercise during the public school day.[13] It appears to be going too far to say that there is such a right. On the other hand, permission for such voluntary practices can be fitted into the concept of accommodation.

The recent decisions touch only marginal aspects of the whole question of religion and the public schools and are negative in character. The really vital question is what the public schools can do in dealing with religion as an appropriate subject of secular education. No one can seriously contend that recognition of the religious element in our national history and a study of religion and of the Bible are inappropriate to public education. It is the end to which such study is directed that is important. In the *Engel* case the court recognized the propriety of using historic national documents and the national anthem to promote patriotism, even though they also reflect religious overtones. More significant, however, was the recognition by the court in *Schempp* that the study of religion in its comparative aspects and of the Bible for its literary and historical value was appropriate to the secular function of the public schools. Any attempt, however, to introduce study about religion and study of the Bible as appropriate secular subjects is accompanied by practical difficulties. How successfully can religion be studied, particularly at the primary level, without inviting the risk of sectarianism and the promotion of particular religious ideas and faiths? No clear answers are indicated, but it is gratifying to see that educators are concerned with this problem, and perhaps it is not too much to hope that something constructive will emerge from the current dialogue. The major religious faiths should work out uses of the Bible and studies of religion that would make meaningful contributions to public education and thereby accord religion the place it rightfully deserves in the public educational scheme.

There is also much discussion of the use of the public schools to promote ethical and moral values. One must approach this subject with caution, for if the purpose is to promote transcendent values and to secure student commitment to these values as essential to our democratic society, the schools may be charged with religious indoctrination. Certainly it is true that for many people moral and ethical values have no religious significance and are unrelated to any belief in God. But for many others religious motivation and faith are the basis of moral and ethical values. They may well object on religious grounds to the teaching of a humanistic ethic. Moreover, if response to ethical imperative is an expression of religious faith, regardless of whether it is founded on belief in a Supreme Being—as held in the recent *Seeger* decision discussed earlier —the objection may be made that the teaching of any ethic is a form of religious instruction and therefore has no place in the public school system. I am not seriously suggesting that courts would sustain this objection and enjoin the teaching of moral values in the public schools, but I mention this to emphasize that in view of the variety of faiths and beliefs of parents whose children are in the public school system, some flexibility and some mutual concessions must be made if the system is to work at all.

This leads to the conclusion that the public schools at most have a very limited function to perform with respect to motivation, commitment, and inculcation of ultimate values. This is not to deny the positive contribution of the public schools in building character and good citizenship. Ethical values and ethical behavior are best promoted by participation in the common life rather than by formal precepts, and in this respect our schools inevitably do much to shape the character of our children, not so much by their formal teaching as by the attitudes and behavior of teachers, the observance of tolerance and respect for human beings, and the promotion of cooperative endeavors that prepare for responsible participation in the life of the community. Moreover, without attempting indoctrination in an officially prescribed system of ethics, the schools can afford opportunity for exploration and discussion of ethical issues and permit a child to give expression to ethical insights derived from his own faith.

Instruction in the religious basis or motivation for ethical conduct is a matter for home and church, and according to the *Zorach* case the public schools may facilitate this kind of instruction by a released time program. This is permissible accommodation of the public school program to presumed religious need. Rather than for the schools to attempt any kind of formal instruction in religion or morality, it is preferable for the schools to recognize that this task belongs to church and the home and within the limits of a released time system to afford opportunity during a prime part of the day for this kind of instruction. The opportunity for released time may be stated in terms broad enough to permit instruction for ethical and moral purposes so as to avoid the charge that this is intended peculiarly for the benefit of parents who want their children instructed in theistic religion and the moral attitudes derived from it. If the state has an appropriate interest in character building and promotion of good citizenship, it should be appropriate for the public school system to permit release of children for the kind of instruction, whether religious or not, which the parents feel most relevant for this purpose.

The subject of religion in public education should not be dismissed without some reference to the study of religion at state-supported colleges and universities. It seems to be generally recognized that the problems of religion in public educational institutions arise particularly in the primary and secondary school systems, and that we enter a wholly different climate of thought and discussion at the level of the state-supported college and university.[14] Without elaborating the arguments in depth, I might mention several primary considerations. In the first place, the fact that education at institutions of higher learning is voluntary sharply distinguishes it from education that is compelled by law. The element of compulsion enters into all the arguments directed against religious instruction in the public schools. Secondly, the fact that courses in religion at state colleges and universities are elective sharply distinguishes them from teaching programs in the public schools, or at least from those at the elementary level. Finally, the greater maturity of students at the college level is a protection against sectarian indoctrination.

No institution can consider itself a genuine college or a university if it ignores the place of religion as an intellectual discipline. The very fact that we have curricula in religion at our state institutions and that the matter continues to be the subject of much study marks an awareness by our educational leaders that religion must find its place in the total educational system. Indeed, it has been persuasively argued that the study

of theology is appropriate to a state institution. No state university can have a theological position any more than it can
have a political position. But just as freedom from a political
position does not preclude a study of political science, so lack
of commitment to a theological position does not preclude
a study of theology. What is important is that the state should
not promote a particular theology for purposes of religious indoctrination, but that rather it should afford opportunity for
study of religious ideas, religious behavior, and religious institutions at the hands of competent scholars. A university offers
the widest latitude to teachers in presenting value systems and
avenues to the pursuit of truth. It is hardly neutral if it denies
opportunity for teaching, research, and study centered on religion in its historical, theological, institutional, and social
aspects.

The second large issue of current concern respecting church-
state relations centers on the interrelationship of government
and churches in areas of overlapping functions. The conception of separation of church and state which rests on the view
that the two institutions have separate functions to perform
and that, therefore, neither should be allowed to intrude into the
other's area of responsibility, does not answer the questions
relating to areas of common concern. Social welfare and education are the two most vital. Churches own and operate hospitals and various welfare institutions such as old folks' homes
and children's homes; they also engage in various types of
social welfare services, such as the care, custody, and placement
of children in cooperation with courts and governmental agencies. Some churches, notably the Roman Catholic church,
operate parochial schools, and various church bodies own and
operate institutions of higher learning.

As pointed out in the first chapter, there has been an expansion of governmental responsibility in these areas and an

enlarged interest by the federal government in the use of its spending power in aid of these enterprises. Under current discussion is the continued role of private voluntaristic organizations in these areas, and the propriety of using governmental funds in their support. Both states and the federal government are spending vast sums in support of expanded health and welfare programs. New demands are placed on the public treasury to provide funds in aid of the educational enterprise at all levels to meet the needs not only of a rapidly expanding school population, but also the demands of a greater proportion of young people for college and professional education. Moreover, the cost of providing health, welfare, and educational services, in response to modern conceptions of adequate facilities, trained personnel, and specialized programs is constantly increasing. It is clear that the major burden of meeting the new demands must be borne by the government. Faced with the expansion of programs financed by public funds and with the growing financial pinch in continuing their own programs in which they are often at a competitive disadvantage, the private institutions are finding it increasingly difficult to maintain their position. The Catholic church, operating the largest church-controlled system of parochial schools, faces a crisis in raising the funds and recruiting the manpower needed for their continued operation. The truth is that many institutions like hospitals and colleges that were once church-related have now ceased virtually to have any connection with the church and have already become quasi-public, in the sense that they rely upon numerous private sources for support or are turning in increasing measure to the government for assistance. The use of government funds to aid the churches in their welfare and educational enterprises precipitates important questions of church-state relations.

It is academic at this point to inquire whether or not the

right to engage in welfare and educational activities is implicit in the concept of religious liberty or essential to the free exercise of religion. A persuasive case can be made to this effect, since these activities do project a distinctively religious motivation and concern. But a broader basis can be found in the general freedom of private voluntaristic enterprise, which finds its constitutional support in the liberty protected by the due process clause. The operation of private schools at the primary and secondary levels introduces a special question of constitutional right, since the parents are free to assert a voice in the education of their children and to make the choice of either public or private school. In the *Pierce* case the Supreme Court, asserting the freedom of parental choice with respect to the education of their children, held unconstitutional a state statute which made it the duty of parents to send their children to the public schools.[15] The court since then has never indicated a retreat from this position. The state may compel parents to send children to a school that meets the state's standards but it must respect the right of parents, if they wish, to send their children to nonpublic schools. The *Pierce* case does not rest so much on the right of private corporations to operate schools as it does on the primary right of parents to make their choice of schools in the education of their children. But it has undeniably large implications for the freedom of parents to send their children to parochial schools and, in turn, for the derivative freedom of the churches to operate these schools.

In meeting the present situation generated by the factors described above, the churches have several alternatives. They may decide to relinquish their interest in welfare and educational enterprises and leave these spheres entirely to the government on the theory that the role of the church in conducting them has become obsolete. They may turn their attention to meeting new and special needs which the government is not prepared to meet. They may decide to continue their present operations in these areas and attempt to meet the financial problem by increased support from their own constituencies or from private benefactors at large. Or, finally, they may turn to the government for such support as it is willing to give. The latter alternative raises issues of church-state relations and the application of the separation principle.

From the viewpoint of the government, is it appropriate to use public funds in aid of church-related enterprises? From the viewpoint of the churches, do they become too deeply involved with government in accepting such assistance and thereby risk the impairment of their voluntaristic position? To some it appears that the answer to the constitutional question is a simple one. Any governmental support of church-related enterprises is in aid of religion and is therefore forbidden by the establishment clause. Others see the problem as far more complex, since it raises questions respecting governmental recognition of the secular purpose served by church-related enterprises, the principle of neutrality, and the freedom of parental choice.

Many of the questions here raised have already come before state courts under provisions of state constitutions. It is a generally accepted constitutional principle whether resting on explicit state constitutional provisions or on judicially developed doctrine that public funds may be expended only for public purposes.[16] In this connection, the further distinction has developed between institutions under public control and those under private control. Some state courts interpret the public purpose limitation to mean that not only must the purpose for which public funds may be spent be a germane public purpose, but that institutions receiving governmental funds must be under public control.[17] Others take the view that spending for a public purpose is permissible even though channeled to institutions not under public control, provided that the legislature imposes such controls or conditions as will insure the achievement of the public purpose or that such controls are inherent in the situation.[18] According to this view public financial support may be extended for a program of service rendered by private institutions, including churches, where the service is seen to confer a public benefit within the competence of the government to provide. But whatever the interpretations arising under state constitutions, it is clear that the distinction between publicly controlled and privately controlled institutions is a familiar one and that no charge of unconstitutional discrimination can be made if a state limits its expenditures for public purposes to institutions under public control. This is a reasonable classification. The religious factor is not relevant to it.

Provisions are also commonly found in state constitutions which forbid appropriations or grants of public funds in aid of religious purposes or of religious corporations or sectarian institutions.[19] Here the religious factor definitely enters into the classification as a basis for special treatment. Under such provisions state courts have invalidated appropriations to church-related hospitals and colleges.[20] Yet some courts have also upheld appropriations or grants to church-related hospitals, on the theory of the purchase by the state of a public service or benefit furnished by the hospital.[21]

Finally, there are provisions commonly found in state constitutions forbidding use of public monies in aid of sectarian education or for the benefit of any theological or religious seminary.[22] Here again the classification is made in terms of the religious factor or a limitation on expenditure of public monies. These provisions have given rise to an extensive body of decisions dealing with such matters as the use of public funds to run public schools that are operated like parochial schools, to provide bus transportation for children to parochial schools, and to provide free textbooks to children in parochial schools. Although courts differ in their interpretation of these provisions, it should be noted that in some instances, particularly in recent cases, the state courts have construed provisions like this to forbid use of public funds to transport children to public schools[23] or to distribute free textbooks to parochial school children.[24] The results rest on the specific provisions of a policy directed against the use of public funds for religious purposes, including sectarian education, and expressly define a constitutional classification based on the religious factor. It is correct, then, to say that these provisions require discrimination on religious grounds in the administration of public monies for public purposes. To say that they are discriminatory in this sense does not necessarily involve condemnation of these provisions. The law is full of classifications that result in preferences and discriminations on various grounds. The point here stressed is that constitutional restrictions on the use of public funds in aid of religious purposes do impose a special disability based on religion.

With regard to these questions raised under the establishment clause of the First Amendment, it should be emphasized that the use of governmental funds to assist religious enterprises raises problems of a distinctive character, compared with other questions respecting religious liberty and church-state relations. Here we are dealing with church-state relations in the direct and authentic sense of the word. The question is one of positive assistance to churches through use of public funds, and the involvement of the government in the affairs of religious institutions stands out conspicuously. It is interesting that Mr. Justice Douglas, who fathered the accommodation theory in the *Zorach* case, has been uncompromising in his objection (expressed in concurring opinions in *Engel*[25] and *Schempp*[26]) to the use of any public funds in support of religious purposes. He seems to think that the idea of accommodation cannot be pushed to the point where it justifies spending in aid of religion. The provisions of the state constitutions mentioned previously also point to a special constitutional tradition against use of public funds to support religious purposes and particularly to support sectarian education.

These complex problems must be separated, and the competing considerations must be weighed in the specific situations that may be involved. Before examining these questions in detail, it should be noted that we already have numerous instances of the use of govermental funds to finance welfare and educational activities in which churches are involved. As mentioned above, in some states public monies are used to help finance welfare services furnished by private agencies, including church-related agencies. More conspicuously, under the federal Hill-Burton Act, grants are made to private hospitals that meet the conditions specified in the statute, including church-related hospitals, and a substantial amount of federal assistance has, in fact, been granted to church-related hospitals under this statute.[27] In the field of higher education, the federal government has granted loans to private colleges, including church-related colleges, in order to enable them to acquire and to build revenue-producing facilities, such as dormitories and cafeterias.[28] Loans to private institutions have been authorized to enable them to acquire special facilities needed to teach science, mathematics, and foreign languages. Only recently, the federal government enacted the first broad aid-to-higher-education bill by authorizing both subsidies and loans to colleges and universities, public and private alike, for the purpose of assisting in the construction of classroom, library, and science laboratory facilities, but with the express limitation that no facilities so acquired shall be used for the teaching of sectarian religion or for the purpose of a divinity hall.[29]

Moreover, substantial financial assistance has been extended to private institutions, including church-related institutions, under the Surplus Property Act, whereby valuable property of various kinds is disposed of by the government at bargain prices.[30] Finally, mention should be made of opportunities extended to church-related institutions, among others, in the acquisition of land pursuant to urban renewal programs. In short, a substantial body of historical practices supports the conclusion that, in the absence of a specific constitutional prohibition, government is not required to discriminate against religious institutions in disbursement of public funds and property pursuant to programs designed to promote the general welfare, and that the separation principle does not preclude the possibility of cooperation between government and the churches in areas of common concern.

Apart from financial assistance extended to church institutions in their corporate capacity, the federal government has pursued programs designed particularly to aid students attending educational institutions, and in these instances has not discriminated against students attending religious institutions. The G.I. benefits made available to all veterans after World War II are a conspicuous illustration. More recently under the National Defense Education Act, the government has made loans available to students attending institutions of higher learning. Again, these benefits are available to students attending private colleges including church-related colleges. Illustrations of this kind of aid may be multiplied.

Situations involving governmental grants or loans to students to enable them to attend college may be put aside, since it is generally conceded that the federal government in exercising its spending power to aid students is not required to discriminate on religious grounds by withholding assistance to students at church-related colleges. This fits the no-aid theory, since the aid is to individuals, and the benefit to the institutions, though it may be real, is incidental. Likewise, such assistance is not only compatible with, but is required by, the neutrality theory.

The more critical questions are raised with respect to grants and loans by the federal government made directly to church-related institutions for hospital and educational purposes. This assistance is extended by the federal government in the exercise of its spending power to promote the general welfare, and the government recognizes that this general welfare is promoted by private as well as public institutions. The private institutions, including church-related hospitals and colleges, are seen to serve a secular purpose. Secondly, these programs are not aimed peculiarly to benefit religious institutions, but are part of a broad program aiding public and private institutions alike. Thirdly, under the Hill-Burton Act and the Higher Education Facilities Act of 1963, the assistance is limited entirely to capital assistance for the purpose of acquiring facilities. Fourthly, some conditions are attached which are designed to assure that these public purposes are served. Under the Hill-Burton Act, hospitals receiving grants are under a duty to maintain the institution as a hospital for at least twenty years, to provide a minimum number of beds for indigent patients, and not to discriminate on the basis of race, creed, or color, unless equal facilities are otherwise available in the area for population groups classified on this basis. It is therefore clear that institutions accepting these grants necessarily accept some limitations on their freedom of action. In terms of constitutional considerations then, the government has proceeded on the theory that in the expenditure of public monies for hospital and higher education purposes, it may recognize lawful secular purposes served by public and private institutions alike in these areas, including church-related institutions, and that it is not required to discriminate against the latter. It has minimized the involvement by government in the private enterprises by limiting the assistance to captial grants but has imposed conditions appropriate to the purposes served by the grants.

Any discussion of the constitutionality of grants or loans to hospitals and educational institutions turns on the application of the no-aid or neutrality theories. The idea of accommodation does not enter into the picture, since it is relevant only when government is acting in distinctive aid of religion. If a strict neutrality theory is followed, the answer to the constitutional problem is readily indicated. By extending aid to all institutions that serve the secular purpose of the government's program, whether public or private, church-related or not, the government is being neutral. Indeed, it would be less than neutral and would be discriminating on religious grounds if it withheld assistance from church-related institutions only. But the no-aid theory raises more questions. If this theory means that government cannot give financial aid in support of religious activities, as distinguished from aid which incidentally benefits religion while advancing a primary secular purpose, then the governmental programs of which we are speaking meet the constitutional test. But if the no-aid principle means that nonpreferential assistance to religious institutions to advance secular purposes may be invalid if government thereby becomes deeply and directly involved in religious matters and if alternative means are available for meeting the public need, no single or categorical answer can be given to our questions.

The constitutionality of grants to church-related hospitals under the Hill-Burton Act raises the least difficulty. Here the secular purpose of promoting and protecting public health is clearly evident. Governmental involvement in religious affairs is at a minimum. No preference is given to any particular religion, and the government imposes only such controls as are necessary to insure that its purpose will be furthered by the grant. It is true that the establishment of a church-related hospital is motivated by religious considerations and that such a hospital may be used to propagate religious views. But medical care and service when extended to patients in a hospital that is open to all can hardly be labeled a form of sectarian indoctrination. Certainly from the viewpoint of the government, the secular and public aspects of the service stand out as the prominent feature. The state court decisions discussed earlier are in accord with this conclusion. Moreover, the community need that must be demonstrated before a grant is made to a hospital under the Hill-Burton Act furnishes strong evidence that the facility is in the public interest.

Leaving aside for the moment grants and loans to colleges, we turn next to the question of governmental aid to parochial schools. The controversy over this problem has helped to stymie any proposal for federal assistance to education at the primary and secondary levels. It is evident that here is the most sensitive issue of church-state relations today. Again, it is clear that if neutrality is the key to the interpretation of the religion clauses of the First Amendment, there would be no problem if the federal government extended aid on an even-handed basis to all schools at the primary and secondary levels, including parochial schools. It is understandable that opponents of federal aid to parochial schools have little use for the neutrality theory. The real issue is joined on the application of the *Everson* no-aid reasoning. Opponents of federal aid to parochial schools argue that such aid would give direct support to religious instruction and hence would amount to an establishment of religion. But the issue cannot be resolved so simply. The actual holding in the *Everson* case was that use of public funds to provide bus transportation for children to parochial schools did not violate the establishment clause. The court recognized that the funds were being spent for a valid secular purpose even though this resulted in an incidental or indirect aid to parochial school education. But it is argued that this does not justify public spending in general aid of parochial schools, since the entire teaching program in these schools is permeated by religion and directed to religious ends and that by supporting this kind of education the state is getting too deeply involved in religious matters. On this point it should be observed that attendance at parochial schools satisfies the requirements of the compulsory education laws. Since these laws are directed to secular ends, it seems clear that the law recognizes the secular aspects of parochial school education. But it is further argued that since all children are free to attend public schools, it is not necessary to support church-operated schools even though they serve an appropriate secular purpose. To accept this argument, however, is to ignore a fundamental aspect of the problem—that parents have a constitutional right to send children to schools of their choice. With the current high cost of maintaining educational facilities and services and the tax burden imposed on all to support public education, the practical effect of denying public funds in support of parochial schools is to seriously abridge the freedom of parents to send their children to nonpublic schools.

This freedom of choice is a highly important value of our democratic society, and in the interest of a benevolent neutrality it should be weighed against the demands of the establishment limitation. It is useful to remember in this connection that the court in its opinion in the *Sherbert* case said that the government should not force a person to violate his religious convictions in order to qualify for financial benefits disbursed under public authority. Taken at its face value this idea is relevant to the parochial school situation.

To state these arguments is to recognize the complexity of the issues. In the absence of an authoritative Supreme Court decision on this question, it is obvious that no categorical opinion can be expressed about it, but that persuasive arguments can be made to refute the frequently expressed view that any aid to parochial schools is forbidden by the establishment clause.[31] Indeed, respectable authorities can be found to support the view that federal aid to parochial schools, as part of a program of aid to all schools, public and private, would be constitutional.[32]

Underlying all these arguments are historic and social policy considerations that may well prove decisive of the result. The historic policy as reflected in state constitutional provisions has been to prohibit sectarian instruction in public schools, to deny the use of public funds in aid of sectarian schools, and in general to limit the use of public educational funds to schools under public control. These historically sanctioned policies relate to the place of the public school in our society as emphasized by Mr. Justice Brennan in his concurring opinion in the *Schempp* case. It is reasonable to anticipate that any program of overall support of private schools—including parochial schools—by public funds would lead to extension and proliferation of private schools, further fragmentizing the educational system and weakening the public schools. Objections may be made that policy formulated in the nineteenth century, when the melting-pot function of the public school system was a particularly vital factor in developing community cohesiveness, is no longer relevant to the present state of American society and should not be engrafted onto the First Amendment in the interpretation of the establishment clause; that our contemporary society is well served by a diversified rather than a monolithic educational structure; and that government support of all schools that meet properly imposed educational standards is the only policy consistent with genuine neutrality and the parental freedom of choice.

The resolution of the constitutional issue as it arises under the First Amendment is not foreclosed by the Supreme Court's prior decisions, and it is hazardous to predict what the court will do with this question if and when the issue is properly presented. I am inclined to think, however, that the use of federal funds to provide overall aid to parochial schools— including support of operating costs (in particular teacher's salaries), even as part of a program in support of all schools— will be declared unconstitutional as a form of aid to religion forbidden by the establishment clause. The established policy, as reflected in state constitutional provisions and practices, against public support of sectarian instruction, and the social policy considerations respecting the public schools will probably carry great weight with the court. The broad dicta in the *Everson* opinion and the holdings in *McCollum* and in the recent prayer and Bible-reading cases all suggest a special judicial sensitivity on the issue of sectarian instruction with the aid of public funds or facilities. It is clear, however, that any such holding would be a decisive repudiation of the neutrality concept in the interpretation of the First Amendment and would have to rest, at least formally, on the proposition that government may not extend nonpreferential assistance in support of secular educational purposes if government thereby substantially involves itself in a program of sectarian instruction.

Yet any conclusion that over-the-board federal assistance to parochial schools would be unconstitutional does not rule out the possibility that assistance geared specially to the secular aspects of their program would be permissible, so far as the federal Constitution is concerned. No one seriously questions the validity of free lunch programs and of health programs administered for the benefit of all school children, including parochial school children. Denial of these benefits to parochial school children would be grossly discriminatory. The Supreme Court has already upheld the constitutionality of using public funds to provide bus transportation for children attending parochial schools and to provide free secular textbooks to children attending all schools, including parochial schools.[33] Likewise, consistent with the denial of support of the overall program which involves substantial elements of religious instruction, the possibility may be open for limited assistance in financing special programs and in acquiring physical facilities and equipment related to such distinctively secular subjects as science, foreign languages, mathematics, and physical education. The federal government already allows deductions under the income tax laws for contributions for religious and educational purposes, the possibility is open for amendment of the tax law to permit deductions for educational expenses.[34] I mention these considerations since the parochial school situation does create a dilemma. Parents have a constitutional right to send their children to parochial schools. The present financial squeeze resulting from the increased burden of taxes to support the public schools—a burden borne by all taxpayers —and the increased difficulty of financing parochial schools may in the end render illusory the constitutional freedom of choice of parents in determining the education of their children. This situation warrents sympathetic consideration by a public that is concerned also with preserving the values of the public school system.

Apart from the possibility of limited aid to parochial schools as suggested above, another proposal that warrants careful study is that of shared time, whereby parochial school children receive a part of their education in distinctively secular subjects such as science and mathematics in facilities owned and operated by the public school authorities. Whether or not such an arrangement is administratively feasible or can be widely adopted remains to be seen. As a creative and constructive plan for integrating all children into the public school system for a part of their education while retaining important elements of education in the parochial schools, it warrants careful exploration.[35] Released time may also be considered as a means of reconciling religious instruction with a program of secular education. It is significant that the Supreme Court to date has not repudiated its decision in the *Zorach* case. Either released time or shared time offers a way out, consistent with maintenance of the secular character of the public school system, for parents who desire religious instruction for their children. There are some discussions within the Catholic church of the desirability of continued maintenance of the parochial school system at all its present levels. If released time or shared time is a viable option for bringing all children, either full-time or part-time, into the public school system, a flexible frame of mind respecting such plans should be entertained. A constructive approach to the parochial school problem requires good will, conciliatory attitudes, and an understanding of all the factors on both sides.

As for the question of federal aid to colleges and universities, including church-related institutions, it is interesting that many who feel very strongly that any assistance to parochial schools would be invalid entertain much more doubt on this question as far as any grants in support of church-related colleges are concerned.[36] Indeed, the Congress that has been stymied over the question of federal aid for education at the primary and secondary levels because of the parochial school problem has only recently enacted a law which provides for grants and subsidies to all colleges and universities, including church-related colleges, for the purpose of acquiring classrooms, li-

braries, and science laboratories.[37] The statute provides that
no such facilities shall be used for the teaching of sectarian
religion or for the purpose of a divinity hall. Congress in
this way has attempted to keep the expenditures within the
limits of what it regards as constitutional requirements. The
question may well be asked why such a marked difference
should be recognized between parochial schools and church-
related colleges. Various arguments are made. First, the federal
purpose involved in aiding higher education cannot be achieved
if the substantial segment represented by private colleges is
disregarded, since at present almost one-half of all students
attending college attend private institutions, whereas by com-
parison only eleven percent of the children enrolled in primary
and secondary schools attend parochial schools. This argument, which assumes varying force depending upon enrollment
statistics, will be weakened as time goes on, since more and
more our public institutions will have to assume the lion's
share of meeting increased demands for college education.

A second argument is that since all children are required
by law to attend primary and secondary schools, governmental
funds should not be used to support parochial schools because
this would support a form of coerced religious instruction.
This argument is not equally relevant to church colleges, since
attendance is voluntary. A further argument is that college
students are more sophisticated and less vulnerable to religious indoctrination, and thus some of the fears entertained
with respect to public support of parochial schools as a means
of sectarian indoctrination are not relevant. This points to
parallel considerations respecting the teaching of religion at
state-supported colleges and universities. Whatever the validity
of these arguments, they evidence a wholly pragmatic approach
to the interpretation of the establishment limitation. Certainly
they do not reflect the application of a rigid no-aid principle.

There is the further problem of distinguishing between private colleges that are church-related and those that are not. What are the tests for determining whether a college is so identifiable with religion that any federal aid to it would be objectionable on the ground that it amounted to support of religion? Should the test be whether a church owns a college, whether the church elects all or a part of the board of trustees of the college, whether chapel services and courses in religion are required, whether a church grants assistance to the institution (and if so, should the degree of assistance be measured), and whether the college is committed by tradition or by its church connection to a given religious faith or ideal? Many institutions which were at one time under strict control by churches no longer have any substantial interrelationship or any distinctive religious orientation. The very difficulty of identifying the criteria for a church-related college and the understandable reluctance of Congress to confide discretionary authority in an administrator to formulate or interpret such criteria are persuasive arguments against singling out one class of private colleges for discriminatory treatment in the granting of federal funds.

In concluding this discussion of public financial support of church-related institutions, I call attention to the risks that these institutions take in subjecting themselves to public control and thereby jeopardizing their freedom and voluntaristic character. Some controls are spelled out in the Hill-Burton Act respecting hospitals and in the Higher Education Facilities Act of 1963. Yet the acceptance of federal assistance may have constitutional significance. In its recent decision in *Simkins v. Moses H. Cone Memorial Hospital,* the United States Court of Appeals of the Fourth Circuit held that a private hospital which received Hill-Burton funds, pursuant to an administrative plan whereby state and federal authorities cooperate in determining community hospital needs and in designating the hospitals to receive the federal grants, had in effect become a state agency and thereby subjected itself to the rule of equal protection under the Fourteenth Amendment.[38] Consequently, it was obliged not to discriminate on the basis of race or color in the admission of patients and doctors.

This decision has implications for all private institutions receiving governmental grants. By accepting grants of governmental funds they subject themselves not only to the controls spelled out in the statute but also to constitutional limitations inherent in their role as state agencies. Whether the doctrine of the *Simkins* case will be approved by the Supreme Court remains to be determined. But if this case is authoritative, many questions are still unanswered. Is acceptance of financial assistance tantamount to constitutional status as a state agency? If so, how much and what kind of financial assistance are necessary for this purpose? Does constitutional status call for the invocation of all constitutional limitations, or is it limited in some special way to basic requirements of the equal protection and due process clauses? How the principle relied on by the court would apply to private colleges and universities receiving grants under the Higher Education Facilities Act of 1963 is not clear. Do such institutions acquire a constitutional status that precludes giving any religious preference in the choice of students and faculty? Does it mean that such institutions may not compel students to take courses with a religious content? Do these institutions by accepting federal grants have the same constitutional position as state colleges and universities? Or will any constitutional status so acquired be adjusted to the special position of educational institutions that serve both secular and religious purposes? One should take care in drawing any conclusion from *Simkins* that goes beyond the problem dealt with in that case. But certainly the decision serves as a warning to church-related institutions that the acceptance of governmental funds invites a possibility of substantial dilution of their voluntaristic position and a secularization of their role and function. The fact that government may have a constitutional basis for furnishing assistance does not answer the question for these institutions of whether the assistance is worth the price they must pay.

The American experiment in religious liberty, buttressed by the separation of church and state, has vindicated itself. The history of religion and of the churches in this country attests to the vitality of the religious life when it depends for its support on spiritual motivation and voluntary adherence, without reliance on the government's coercive power. But a regard for the separation principle should not obscure the fundamental consideration that there is a necessary interdependence of religion and government, that religion and the churches have a role to play with respect to the public order and the common life, that government has a role to perform in the protection and advancement of religious liberty, and that government and the churches share some overlapping concerns and functions.

The religious, social, and political movements in American life call for fresh appraisal of the meaning of religious liberty and the separation principle with regard to the problems we face today. These problems, respecting religion and the constitutional order, are not solved by an uncritical invocation of slogans or rigid dogmas. They call for analysis and understanding of the varieties of interests involved and for a judgment that is informed by appreciation of a complex of fundamental values served by our constitutional system in implementing the goals of a free society. We are dealing with basic policy considerations which depend for their ultimate validity and sanction, not on the decisions and opinions of the courts, but on the consensus established by a public informed by debate and discussion. To bring fresh, creative, critical, and constructive thought to bear in the establishment of this consensus is the responsibility and the task with which we are challenged.

NOTES

Chapter 1

1 Abington School District v. Schempp, 374 U.S. 203 (1963); Murray v. Curlett, 374 U.S. 203 (1963).

2 See Littell, *From State Church to Pluralism*, 129–69; Marty, *The New Shape of American Religion*, 1–5; Niebuhr, "The Religious Situation in America," in Stahmer (ed.), *Religion and Contemporary Society*.

3 See *Relations Between Church and State in the United States of America*, a report adopted by the 175th General Assembly of the United Presbyterian Church in the U.S.A. (May, 1963); *Church and State—A Lutheran Perspective*, a report by the Commission on Church and State Relations in a Pluralistic Society, under the auspices of the Board of Social Ministry—Lutheran Church in America (1963).

Chapter 2

1 U.S. Const. amend. I.

2 *E.g.*, Ga. Const. art. 1, §1, ¶ 12; Kan. Const. art. 1, §7;

La. Const. art. 1, §4; Me. Const. art. 1, §3; N. H. Const. Part I, art. 5; So. Dak. Const. art. 2, §3; Wis. Const. art. 1, §18.

3 *E.g.*, Ill. Const. art. 2, §3; Mich. Const. art. 1, §§ 2, 4; N. J. Const. art. 1, §5; Vt. Const. chap. I, art. 3.

4 *E.g.*, Del. Const. art. 1, §1; Ky. Const., Bill of Rights, §5; Md. Const., Declaration of Rights, art. 36; Minn. Const. art. 1, §16; N. J. Const. art. 1, ¶ 3; Ohio Const. art. 1, §7; Va. Const. art. 4, §58.

5 *E.g.*, Ariz. Const. art. 11, §7; Mont. Const. art. 11, §9; Neb. Const. art. 7, §11; Nev. Const. art. 11, §9; So. Dak. Const. art. 8, §16; Wis. Const. art. 10, §3; Wyo. Const. art. 7, §12.

6 *E.g.*, Cal. Const. art. 4, §30; Hawaii Const. art. 9, §1; Ill. Const. art 8, §3; Minn. Const. art. 8, §2; N. M. Const. art. 12, §3; N. Y. Const. art. 11, §3; Pa. Const. art. 3, §18, art. 10, §2; Tex. Const. art. 1, §7; Wyo. Const. art. 1, §19, art. 3, §36, art. 7, §8.

7 West Virginia State Board of Educ. v. Barnette, 319 U.S. 624 (1943).

8 Kurland, *Religion and the Law*, 16–18.

9 See, *e.g.*, Follett v. Town of McCormick, 321 U. S. 573 (1944); Murdock v. Pennsylvania, 319 U. S. 105 (1943); Cantwell v. Connecticut, 310 U.S. 296 (1940).

10 *E.g.*, Ill. Const. art. 9, §3; Mich. Const. art. 9, §4; N. Y. Const. art. 16, §1; Pa. Const. art. 9, §1; Tex. Const. art. 8, §2.

11 Paulsen, "Preferment of Religious Institutions in Tax and Labor Legislation," *Law & Contemp. Prob.*, XIV (1949), 144.

12 See note 6 *supra*.

13 See Harfst v. Hoegen, 349 Mo. 808, 163 S.W.2d 609 (1941); Zellers v. Huff, 55 N. Mex. 501, 236 P.2d 949 (1951).

14 Dickman v. School District, 223 Ore. 366, 366 P.2d 533 (1961).

15 Reynolds v. Nusbaum, 17 Wis. 2d 148, 115 N.W.2d 761 (1962); Visser v. Nooksack Valley School District, 33 Wash. 2d 699, 207 P.2d 198 (1949).

16 Fowler v. Rhode Island, 345 U. S. 67 (1953); Niemotko v. Maryland, 340 U.S. 268, 284 (1951) (Frankfurter concurring).

17 Jamison v. Texas, 318 U. S. 413 (1943); Schneider v. State,

308 U. S. 147 (1939); Lovell v. Griffin, 303 U.S. 444 (1938).

18 Marsh v. Alabama, 326 U. S. 501 (1946); Follett v. Town of McCormick, 321 U. S. 573 (1944); Murdock v. Pennsylvania, 319 U. S. 105 (1943).

19 Compare Martin v. City of Struthers, 319 U. S. 141 (1943) (restriction on door-to-door distribution of religious tracts prohibited) with Breard v. Alexandria, 341 U. S. 622 (1951) (restriction on door-to-door solicitation of magazine subscriptions upheld); compare Jamison v. Texas, 318 U. S. 413 (1943) (restriction on distribution of religious tracts on city streets prohibited) with Valentine v. Christensen, 316 U. S. 52 (1942) (restriction on distribution of commercial handbills on city streets upheld).

20 Murdock v. Pennsylvania, 319 U. S. 105 (1943).

21 See note 19 *supra.*

22 374 U. S. 398 (1963).

23 See, *e.g.,* Constitution of Japan, art. 20; Basic Law for the Federal Republic of Germany art. 4; Constitution of the Italian Republic art. 19, 20.

24 See generally, Bates, *Religious Liberty,* 378–475; Bennett, *Christians and the State,* 130–62; de Albornoz, *The Basis of Religious Liberty,* 15–98; Pfeffer, *Church, State, and Freedom,* 81–93.

25 See his dissenting opinion in Abrams v. United States, 250 U. S. 616, 624 (1919).

26 Meiklejohn, *Political Freedom,* 24–28.

27 De Albornoz, *The Basis of Religious Liberty,* 16–19.

28 First Assembly of the World Council of Churches, Amsterdam, 1948, Report on "The Church and the Disorder of Society" (cited in de Albornoz, *The Basis of Religious Liberty,* 133–41).

29 Acts, 5:29.

30 See Bennett, *Christians and the State,* 137–40.

31 Bates, *Religious Liberty,* 432–68; Brown and Weigel, *An American Dialogue,* 58–66.

32 Bates, *Religious Liberty,* 403–407; Pfeffer, *Church, State, and Freedom,* 80–102.

33 See symposium by Ball, Cross, Konvitz, Powell, Pfeffer, Shinn and Whelan, "The Meaning of Religion in the First Amend-

ment," *Catholic World* (Aug., 1963); Stahmer, "Defining Religion," in Giannella (ed.), *1963 Religion and the Public Order,* 116.

34 Murdock v. Pennsylvania, 319 U. S. 105 (1943).

35 Lovell v. Griffin, 303 U. S. 444 (1938).

36 Niemotko v. Maryland, 340 U. S. 268 (1951).

37 Torcaso v. Watkins, 367 U. S. 488 (1961).

38 West Virginia State Board of Educ. v. Barnette, 319 U. S. 624 (1943).

39 Kedroff v. St. Nicholas Cathedral, 344 U. S. 94 (1952).

40 310 U. S. 296 (1940).

41 322 U. S. 78 (1944).

42 *Ibid.,* 95.

43 50 U.S.C. §456.

44 50 U.S.C. §456(j).

45 133 U. S. 333 (1890).

46 *Ibid.,* 342.

47 United States v. Macintosh, 283 U. S. 605, 633–34 (1931).

48 367 U. S. 488 (1961).

49 *Ibid.,* 495.

50 *Ibid.,* 495 n. 11.

51 326 F.2d 846 (2d Cir. 1964).

52 133 F.2d 703, 708 (2d Cir. 1943).

53 Abington School Dist. v. Schempp, 374 U. S. 203 (1963); Engel v. Vitale, 370 U. S. 421 (1962).

54 Abington School Dist. v. Schempp, 374 U. S. 203, 313 (1963) (Stewart dissenting).

55 This test was proposed by the Rev. Dean Kelley of the National Council of Churches. See symposium by Ball *et al.,* "The Meaning of Religion in the First Amendment," *Catholic World* (Aug., 1963), 316.

56 United States v. Jakobson, 325 F.2d 409 (2d Cir. 1963).

57 See text and accompanying footnotes pp. 19, 20 *supra.*

58 *E.g.,* Constitution of India art. 25, §§25, 26; Constitution of Ireland art. 44, §§1, 2; Basic Law for the Federal Republic of Germany art. 4, Weimar Constitution art. 137.

59 St. Nicholas Cathedral v. Kreshnik, 363 U. S. 190 (1960); Kedroff v. St. Nicholas Cathedral, 344 U. S. 94 (1952).

60 Va. Const. art. 4, §59.

61 W. Va. Const. art. 6, §47.

62 See note 59 *supra*.

63 Cantwell v. Connecticut, 310 U. S. 296, 303–304 (1940).

64 Jacobson v. Massachusetts, 197 U. S. 11 (1905).

65 Chaplinsky v. New Hampshire, 315 U. S. 568 (1942).

66 Prince v. Massachusetts, 321 U. S. 158 (1944).

67 Reynolds v. United States, 98 U. S. 145 (1878).

68 Corporation of the Presiding Bishop of the Church of Jesus Christ of Latter Day Saints v. City of Porterville, 90 Cal. App. 2d 656, 203 P.2d 823, appeal dismissed for want of a substantial federal question, 338 U. S. 805 (1949).

69 Schenck v. United States, 249 U. S. 47 (1919).

70 See Kauper, *Frontiers of Constitutional Liberty*, 111–12.

71 See Kauper, "The Constitutionality of Tax Exemptions for Religious Activities," in Oaks (ed.), *The Wall Between Church and State*, 95.

72 See Paulsen, "Preferment of Religious Institutions in Tax and Labor Legislation," *Law & Contemp. Prob.*, XIV (1949), 144.

73 50 U.S.C. §456.

74 See listing of statutes in Mr. Justice Frankfurter's concurring opinion in McGowan v. Maryland, 366 U. S. 420, 515 n. 103 (1961).

75 See note 18 *supra*.

76 See note 19 *supra*.

77 Braunfeld v. Brown, 366 U. S. 599 (1961).

78 Sherbert v. Verner, 374 U. S. 398 (1963). Since the statute recognized the privilege of not accepting a Sunday job where work on Sunday offended religious belief, the case might have rested on the ground of discrimination, but the court chose to rest its decision on a broader basis.

Chapter 3

1 Reynolds v. United States, 98 U. S. 145, 164 (1878).

2 Engel v. Vitale, 370 U. S. 421, 436 (1962).

3 Brant, *James Madison*, 271–75.

4 Stokes, *Church and State in the United States*, I, 543–49.

5 Abington School Dist. v. Schempp, 374 U. S. 203, 234–36 (1963).

6 Page 14 *supra*.

7 See generally, Torpey, *Judicial Doctrines of Religious Rights in America*, chap. 1.

8 New York Trust Co. v. Eisner, 256 U. S. 345, 349 (1921).

9 Jackman v. Rosenbaum Co., 260 U. S. 22, 31 (1922).

10 McCollum v. Board of Education, 333 U. S. 203, 216 (1948).

11 Bradfield v. Roberts, 175 U. S. 291 (1899). See also Quick Bear v. Leupp, 210 U. S. 50 (1908).

12 Everson v. Board of Education, 330 U. S. 1 (1947).

13 *Sub nom.* Massachusetts v. Mellon, 262 U. S. 447 (1923).

14 See note 6, chap. 2 *supra*.

15 McCollum v. Board of Education, 333 U. S. 203 (1948).

16 Zorach v. Clauson, 343 U. S. 306 (1952).

17 McGowan v. Maryland, 366 U. S. 420 (1961); Two Guys from Harrison-Allentown, Inc. v. McGinley, 366 U. S. 582 (1961); Gallagher v. Crown Kosher Super Market Inc., 366 U. S. 619 (1961); Braunfeld v. Brown, 366 U. S. 599 (1961).

18 Engel v. Vitale, 370 U. S. 421 (1962). For the author's previous discussion of this case see Kauper, "Prayer, Public Schools and the Supreme Court," *Mich. L. Rev.*, LXI (1963), 1031.

19 Abington School Dist. v. Schempp, 374 U. S. 203 (1963).

20 See Adamson v. California, 332 U. S. 46 (1947) and dissenting opinion by Mr. Justice Black, *ibid.*, 68.

21 Palko v. Connecticut, 302 U. S. 319 (1937).

22 See generally, Kauper, "Prayer, Public Schools and the Supreme Court," *Mich. L. Rev.*, LXI (1963), 1031, 1058–60.

23 Abington School Dist. v. Schempp, 374 U. S. 203, 310 (1963).

24 See note 10 *supra*.

25 374 U. S. 203, 254–58.

26 *Ibid.*, 217.

27 Page 53 *supra*.

28 For general discussions of the standing problem see Brown, *"Quis Custodiet Ipsos Custodes?*—The School Prayer Cases," *Supreme Court Rev.* (1963), 1; Sutherland, "Establishment According to Engel," *Harv. L. Rev.*, LXXVI (1962), 25.

29 Everson v. Board of Education, 330 U. S. 1, 15–16 (1947).

30 McCollum v. Board of Education, 333 U. S. 203 (1948).

31 Engel v. Vitale, 370 U. S. 421 (1962).

32 330 U. S. 18 (Jackson dissenting; Frankfurter joining); *ibid.*, 28 (Rutledge dissenting; Frankfurter, Jackson, Burton joining).

33 See note 17 *supra.*

34 Abington School Dist. v. Schempp, 374 U. S. 203 (1963). See Kauper "Schempp and Sherbert: Studies in Neutrality and Accommodation," in Giannella (ed.), *1963 Religion and the Public Order*, 3.

35 374 U. S. 203, 222.

36 Kurland, *Religion and the Law*, 16–18. For a criticism of Kurland's thesis, see Konvitz, "The Constitution or Neutral Principles," in Giannella (ed.), *1963 Religion and the Public Order*, 99.

37 Zorach v. Clauson, 343 U. S. 306, 314 (1952).

38 374 U. S. 203, 229.

39 Katz, "Freedom of Religion and State Neutrality," *U. Chi. L. Rev.*, XX (1953), 426.

40 343 U. S. 306 (1952).

41 343 U. S. 306, 315 (Black dissenting); *ibid.*, 320 (Frankfurter dissenting); *ibid.*, 323 (Jackson dissenting).

42 Kauper, *Civil Liberties and the Constitution*, 15–19; Kurland, *Religion and the Law*, 86–90; Jones, "Church-State Relations: Our Constitutional Heritage," in Stahmer (ed.), *Religion and Contemporary Society*, 190.

43 343 U. S. 306, 312–14.

44 Katz, "Freedom of Religion and State Neutrality," *U. Chi. L. Rev.*, XX (1953), 426.

45 374 U. S. 203, 230–304.

46 *Ibid.*, 305–308.

47 370 U. S. 421, 444–50.

48 374 U. S. 203, 308–320.

49 Sherbert v. Verner, 374 U. S. 398 (1963).

50 *Ibid.*, 413–18.

51 *Ibid.*, 418–23.

Chapter 4

1 See Littell, *From State Church to Pluralism*, 120–25; Pfeffer, *Church, State and Freedom*, 192–206.

2 Zorach v. Clauson, 343 U. S. 306, 314 (1952).

3 See "A Dialogue on Church and State," published by Indiana Area of the Methodist Church (1963), p. 17.

4 West Virginia Board of Education v. Barnette, 319 U. S. 624, 642 (1943).

5 McCollum v. Board of Education, 333 U. S. 203 (1948).

6 Abington School Dist. v. Schempp, 374 U. S. 203 (1963); Murray v. Curlett, 374 U. S. 203 (1963).

7 The decision in Torcaso v. Watkins, 367 U. S. 488 (1961), holding that a state could not require an affirmation of belief in God as a condition of taking public office, might well have rested on the establishment clause, but the actual ground for decision was that such a requirement was a violation of religious liberty. *Torcaso* is a case where the free exercise and establishment clauses converge on the same result.

8 374 U. S. 203, 260–62.

9 Indeed, one writer has suggested that the public schools be given responsibility for teaching democracy as religion. See Williams, *What Americans Believe and How They Worship*, 368, 371, 373.

10 Johnson and Yost, *Separation of Church and State in the United States*, 17–31; Pfeffer, *Church, State, and Freedom*, 274–86.

11 374 U. S. 203, 307 (Goldberg concurring); *ibid.*, 294–99 (Brennan concurring).

12 McCollum v. Board of Education, 333 U. S. 203, 232 (1948).

13 Stein v. Oshinsky, 224 F. Supp. 757 (E.D., N. Y. 1963). The court upheld the constitutional right of kindergarten children of various religious faiths to engage in voluntary prayer and issued an order to the school officials to afford the children opportunity for such prayer, subject to reasonable rules and regulations to be prescribed by the school authorities.

14 See generally, McLean and Kimber, *The Teaching of Religion in State Universities;* Kauper, "Law and Public Opinion," in Walter (ed.), *Religion and the State University,* 69; Louisell and Jackson, "Religion, Theology, and Public Higher Education," *Calif. L. Rev.,* L (1962), 751.

15 Pierce v. Society of Sisters, 268 U. S. 510 (1925).

16 For general discussions of the public purpose doctrine, see Judson, "Public Purposes for Which Taxation Is Justifiable," *Yale L. J.* XVII (1907), 162; Kneier, "Municipal Functions and the Law of Public Purpose," *U. Pa. L. Rev.,* LXXVI (1928), 824; McAllister, "Public Purpose in Taxation," *Calif. L. Rev.,* XVIII (1929), 137, 241. For a recent judicial review of the doctrine, see City of Frostburg v. Jenkins, 215 Md. 9, 136 A. 2d 852 (1957).

17 See, *e.g.,* Detroit Museum of Art. v. Engel, 187 Mich. 432, 153 N. W. 700 (1915).

18 See, *e.g.,* Craig v. Mercy Hospital, 209 Miss. 427, 45 So.2d, 809 (1950); Kentucky Bldg. Commission v. Effron, 310 Ky. 355, 220 S.W.2nd 836 (1949). See also City of Frostburg v. Jenkins, note 16 *supra.*

19 See, *e.g.,* Calif. Const. art. 4, §30; Mont. Const. art. 5, §35; Va. Const. art. 4, §67.

20 Bennett v. LaGrange, 153 Ga. 428, 112 S. E. 482 (1922); Cook County v. Chicago Industrial School, 125 Ill. 540, 18 N.E. 183 (1888); Collins v. Kephart, 271 Pa. 428, 117 A. 2d 470 (1921); Synod of Dakota v. State, 2 S. Dak. 366, 50 N.W. 632 (1891).

21 See Craig v. Mercy Hospital, note 18 *supra;* Kentucky Bldg. Commission v. Effron, note 18 *supra;* Schade v. Allegheny County, 386 Pa. 507, 126 A.2d 911 (1956).

22 See chap. 2, note 6 *supra.*

23 For recent decisions to this effect, see Board of Education v. Antone, 384, P.2d 911 (Okla. 1963); Reynolds v. Nusbaum, 17 Wis.2d 148, 115 N.W.2d 761 (1962).

24 For a recent decision, see Dickman v. School District, 223 Ore. 366, P.2d 533 (1961).

25 370 U.S. 421, 437.

26 374 U. S. 203, 227.

27 42 U. S. C. §§291 (a)-(n).

28 Under authority of Title IX of the Housing Act of 1950, 64 Stat. 77, as amended, 12 U. S. C. §1749.

29 20 U. S. C. A. §§701–57.

30 40 U. S. C. §§484 (j),(k). See memorandum by General Counsel of Department of Health, Education, and Welfare, in *Constitutionality of Federal Aid to Education in Various Aspects,* p. 23, n. 18, Sen. Doc. No. 29, 87th Cong., 1st Sess., suggesting that this program transgresses constitutional boundaries.

31 Gordon, "The Unconstitutionality of Public Aid to Parochial Schools," in Oaks (ed.), *The Wall Between Church and State,* 73; Konvitz, "Separation of Church and State, The First Freedom," *Law & Contemp. Prob.,* XIV (1949), 44; Pfeffer, "The Case for Separation," in Cogley (ed.), *Religion in America,* 52.

32 See Drinan, "The Constitutionality of Public Aid to Parochial Schools," in Oaks (ed.), *The Wall Between Church and State,* 55; Katz, "The Case for Religion Liberty," in Cogley (ed.), *Religion in America,* 109; Kurland, *Religion and the Law,* 9.

33 Everson v. Board of Education, 330 U. S. 1 (1947) (bus transportation); Cochran v. Louisiana State Board of Education, 281 U. S. 370 (1930) (textbooks). The establishment question was not at issue in the *Cochran* case.

34 Int. Rev. Code of 1954, §170.

35 See "Shared Time: A Symposium," *Religious Education* (Jan.-Feb., 1962); also La Noue, *Pioneer Ideas in Education* (Background Report published by National Conference of Christians and Jews, 1964).

36 Memorandum by General Counsel of Department of Health, Education, and Welfare (*supra* note 30), 24; Pfeffer, *Church, State, and Freedom,* 423.

37 20 U. S. C. A. §§701–57.

38 323 F.2d 959 (4th Cir. 1963).

SELECTED BIBLIOGRAPHY

BOOKS

Bates, Ernest E. *American Faith: Its Religious, Political, and Economic Foundations.* New York: Norton & Co., 1940.

Bates, M. Searle. *Religious Liberty: An Inquiry.* New York: Harper & Bros., 1945.

Bennett, John C. *Christians and the State.* New York: Charles Scribner's Sons, 1958.

Brant, Irving. *James Madison: Father of the Constitution, 1787–1800.* New York: Bobbs-Merrill Co., 1950.

Brown, Robert McAfee, and Gustave Weigel, S.J. *An American Dialogue.* Garden City, N. Y.: Doubleday paperback ed., 1961.

Cogley, John (ed.). *Religion in America: Original Essays on Religion in a Free Society.* New York: Meridian paperback ed., 1958.

Costanzo, Joseph, S.J. *This Nation Under God: Church, State and*

Schools in America. New York: Herder and Herder, 1964.

De Albornoz, A. F. Carrillo. *The Basis of Religious Liberty.* New York: Association Press, 1963.

Drinan, Robert F., S.J. *Religion, the Courts, and Public Policy.* New York: McGraw-Hill Book Co., 1963.

Freund, Lally, Hook, Eisendrath, Corson, Littell. *A Dialogue on Church and State.* Indianapolis: Indiana Area of the Methodist Church, 1963.

Giannella, Donald A. (ed.). *1963 Religion and the Public Order: An Annual Review of Church and State and of Religion, Law, and Society.* Chicago: University of Chicago Press, 1964.

Herberg, Will. *Protestant, Catholic, Jew: An Essay in American Religious Sociology.* Garden City, N. Y.: Doubleday paperback ed., 1960.

Johnson, Alvin W., and Frank H. Yost. *Separation of Church and State in the United States.* Minneapolis: University of Minnesota Press, 1948.

Katz, Wilber G. *Religion and American Constitutions.* Evanston: Northwestern University Press, 1964.

Kauper, Paul G. *Civil Liberties and the Constitution.* Ann Arbor: University of Michigan Press, 1962. See esp. chap. 1.

—————. *Frontiers of Constitutional Liberty.* Ann Arbor: University of Michigan Law School, 1956. See esp. chap. 3.

Kurland, Philip B. *Religion and the Law: Of Church and State and the Supreme Court.* Chicago: Aldine Pub. Co., 1962.

Littell, Franklin Hamlin. *From State Church to Pluralism: A Protestant Interpretation of Religion in American History.* Garden City, N. Y.: Doubleday paperback ed., 1962.

Marty, Martin E. *The New Shape of American Religion.* New York: Harper & Bros., 1959.

McLean, Milton D., and Harry H. Kimber. *The Teaching of Religion in State Universities.* Ann Arbor: University of Michigan Office of Religious Affairs, 1960.

Meiklejohn, Alexander. *Political Freedom: The Constitutional Powers of the People.* New York: Harper & Bros., 1960.

Murray. John Courtney, S.J. *We Hold These Truths: Catholic Reflections on the American Proposition.* New York: Sheed and Ward, 1960.

Oaks, Dallin H. (ed.). *The Wall Between Church and State.* Chicago: University of Chicago Press, 1963.

Pfeffer, Leo. *Church, State, and Freedom.* Boston: Beacon Press, 1953.

Stahmer, Harold (ed.). *Religion and Contemporary Society.* New York: Macmillan Co., 1963.

Stokes, Anson Phelps. *Church and State in the United States.* 3 vols. New York: Harper & Bros., 1950.

Torpey, William G. *Judicial Doctrines of Religious Rights in America.* Chapel Hill: University of North Carolina Press, 1948.

Walter, Erich A. (ed.). *Religion and the State University.* Ann Arbor: University of Michigan Press, 1958.

PERIODICAL ARTICLES

Ball, Cross, Konvitz, Powell, Pfeffer, Shinn and Whelan. "The Meaning of Religion in the First Amendment," *Catholic World* (August, 1963), 280.

Brown, Ernest J. *"Quis Custodiet Ipsos Custodes?*—The School-Prayer Cases," *Supreme Court Review* (1963), 1.

Cahn, Edmond. "The 'Establishment of Religion' Puzzle," *New York University Law Review* XXXVII (1961), 1274.

——————————. "On Government and Prayer," *New York University Law Review*, XXXVII (1962), 981

Choper, Jesse H. "Religion in the Public Schools: A Proposed Constitutional Standard," *Minnesota Law Review*, XLVII (1963), 329.

Corwin, Murray, Konvitz, Meiklejohn, Fahy, Sullivan, Mitchell, Paulsen. "Symposium—Religion and the State," *Law and Contemporary Problems*, XIV (1949), 3.

Katz, Wilber G. "Freedom of Religion and State Neutrality." *University of Chicago Law Review*, XX (1953), 426.

Kauper, Paul G. "Prayer, Public Schools and the Supreme Court," *Michigan Law Review*, LXI (1963), 1031.

——————————. "Church and State: Cooperative Separatism," *Michigan Law Review*, LXI (1961), 1.

Kurland, Philip B. "The Regents' Prayer Case: 'Full of Sound and Fury, Signifying . . . ,' " *Supreme Court Review* (1962), 1.

Louisell, David W., and John H. Jackson. "Religion, Theology, and Public Higher Education," *California Law Review*, L (1962), 751.

Pfeffer, Leo. "Court, Constitution and Prayer," *Rutgers Law Review*, XVI (1962), 735.

——————————. "Some Current Issues in Church and State," *Western Reserve Law Review*, XIII (1961), 9.

Sutherland, Arthur E., Jr. "Establishment According to Engel," *Harvard Law Review*, LXXVI (1962), 25.

——————————. "Due Process and Disestablishment," *Harvard Law Review* LXII (1949), 1306.

Van Alstyne, William W. "Constitutional Separation of Church and State: The Quest For a Coherent Position." *American Political Science Review*, LVII (1963), 865.

TABLE OF CASES